MW00888271

Just Behind the Door

Communicating With Our Loved Ones Who Have Passed On

MARY LEIKER

authorHOUSE®

AuthorHouse™
1663 Liberty Drive
Bloomington, IN 47403
www.authorhouse.com
Phone: 1-800-839-8640

© *2012 Mary Leiker. All rights reserved.*

No part of this book may be reproduced, stored in a retrieval system, or transmitted by any means without the written permission of the author.

Published by AuthorHouse 4/12/2012

ISBN: 978-1-4685-6227-9 (e)
ISBN: 978-1-4685-6228-6 (hc)
ISBN: 978-1-4685-6229-3 (sc)

Library of Congress Control Number: 2012904705

Any people depicted in stock imagery provided by Thinkstock are models, and such images are being used for illustrative purposes only. Certain stock imagery © *Thinkstock.*

This book is printed on acid-free paper.

Because of the dynamic nature of the Internet, any web addresses or links contained in this book may have changed since publication and may no longer be valid. The views expressed in this work are solely those of the author and do not necessarily reflect the views of the publisher, and the publisher hereby disclaims any responsibility for them.

Dedication

To my family on the other side — Ronnie, Mom and Phyllis — you are so loved. Your inspiration and insistence that I commit to writing about our on-going communication has been a journey for me into areas that stretched my abilities beyond my wildest expectations. At times I have felt I was simply 'not encumbered' by the thought process and then you would come through, yet again, to enlighten me. You are the sun, moon and stars to me. Thank you for never letting go. I know you are always with me and I am humbled by your belief in me.

To Zach, you are the light in my life! You are love and light, an old soul who never fails to amaze me with your heart, incredible gifts and panache. The universe was in perfect alignment when you were born. How fortunate I am that you chose me as your mother.

To my family on this side, Barbie, Carolyn, Suzie, Lois, and friends, Carole, MS, and Lee, you are my sounding board, my teachers and my greatest cheerleaders. You see things in me that I hope someday to become. Thank you for always being there for me.

To Ryan, Jake and J.T., I love you so much. Always remember that your Dad is with you, around you and in you. He is only a thought away. Simply open the doors of your mind and he will be there to guide, protect and show you his everlasting love.

To Gina, thank you for giving Ronnie the greatest gift in his life, the wonder of true love and blessing of children.

ML

Contents

To Those Whom I Love and Those Who Love Me

When I am gone, release me, let me go.
I have so many things to see and do,
You must not tie yourself to me with too many tears,
But be thankful we had so many good years.
I gave you my love, and you can only guess
How much you've given me in happiness.
I thank you for the love that you have shown,
But now it is time I traveled on alone.
So grieve for me a while, if grieve you must,
Then let your grief be comforted by trust.
It is only for a while that we must part,
So treasure the memories within your heart.
I won't be far away for life goes on.
And if you need me, call and I will come.
Though you can't see or touch me, I will be near.
And if you listen with your heart, you will hear,
All my love around you soft and clear.
And then when you come this way alone,
I'll greet you with a smile and a 'Welcome Home.' Anon

Introduction

Letting go does not mean to forget, the definition of that word is simply, "not being able to remember." Who would we be kidding? Not being able to remember our loved ones who have passed on, impossible! Losing my son, mom, dad, sisters, husbands, and best friends have taught me so much about letting go. It has been a difficult and arduous journey. Along the way I have learned how to communicate with these loved ones. I share my story with you in the hope that you will find a measure of peace, consider the possibility of reconnecting with your loved ones, and gain a renewed sense of purpose in your life after the most devastating experience imaginable, the loss of your loved one.

What would that special person want you to do with your grief? Would they want you to create a memorial in your home, stop living in the here-and-now and freeze-frame your life at the moment they passed on? I am absolutely certain that they would not since that would impede your own life lessons and is not productive or healthy. In fact, your loved one now possesses a much greater understanding of life. Since passing over they have the gift of greater knowing, a heightened sense of purpose and a deeper understanding about the journey of life. They see, feel, hear, and know on a level beyond our ability to even conceptualize. Of course, they want us to keep the memories alive of the love, the good times and even the challenges we had with them. They want to continue to be a healthy part of our lives. Most importantly, they want us to hear them when they communicate to us. I know this because I have experienced this communication for over a decade.

If your loved one was still alive and went on vacation, you would not stop living or become paralyzed until their return. That is dysfunctional.

My son who has passed on told me specifically to think of his physical absence as a move for him to a different location. He has repeatedly assured me that he is still with me and lovingly communicates with me to help me in my life journey. As he has often said, *"Don't say good-bye just say see you later because you will."*

Sometimes we are so afraid of forgetting that we hold onto the trauma of the loss of our loved one for the rest of our lives. It would be similar to holding onto a life raft. At first you may need it to survive, it is a necessity. When the waters are stormy and the boat has just capsized, you need the raft to save yourself. But when the life raft meets the shore and the water is calmer, it no longer helps you. In fact, it becomes an impediment to carry through life. Your grief, anger or fear is like the life raft that has reached the shore. If you hold on to it you will be prevented from moving forward with your own life script.

This book is about helping people reach the shore and learn to let go of the raft, no matter how long ago your loss took place. It is about showing you how to communicate with your loved one who may be gone from this earth plane but is right behind the door.

It is so important to live one day at a time. To be present in everything the world has to offer and to work to regain, a sense of wonder, possibility and love after a personal loss. We all experience difficult days and think, "Will this ever end?" Depression — true depression — can sap the life force right out of you. It can cause you to become a shell of the person you once were. There is research that shows how continual depression can actually change your brain function. There are people who have actual chemical imbalances in their system. Depression, panic attacks as well as other debilitating conditions are part of their everyday lives. However, there are others who experience depression after a loss in their life and it is totally foreign to them. They are at first puzzled, then fearful of it, and finally resigned that it simply will not leave them. Depression that sets in after the loss of a loved one is part of the grieving process. It is natural. The length of time that the depression remains is the issue to honestly examine.

No one will be helped, nothing will be changed and the loss will not be reversed by the ongoing depression you may be feeling. In fact, your life work, the reason you are here, will be interrupted. Your very being will be altered and you will become stuck in that never — never land of "why." I know how hard it is to move past the depression. You can't simply snap your fingers and say, "today I will not be depressed." However, recognizing the depression for what it is must be the first step in getting through it. Holding on to blame, anger or the "what ifs" (if I had been with him he would not have died; if I had kept him on the phone longer, it could have been prevented, or if we would have sought out other medical treatment, she would not have died) are all ways that keep us in denial, pain, anger and depression. They take a frightening toll on your body. Disease is just as it sounds: dis-ease. Your body is not at ease, not in sync. Just like any system, when it is out of balance, over time, different parts of the system will gradually break down. Our bodies are a system of energy that relies on proper circuitry to maintain both a healthy body and mind.

I have been able to communicate with my son and mother for a decade and my sister for seven years. Yes, they are right behind the door. They are with me through "thick and thin" as my mother would say. You can also get to this point in your life. I am living proof that it is real.

According to Rudolf Calusius in 1850, energy can neither be created nor destroyed. Elaborating on his premise, the First Law of Thermodynamics states, "Energy can be transformed but cannot be created nor destroyed." This is an extremely important scientific theory to wrap your mind around as you read this book. So, if the shell — the body — is gone, where is the energy, spirit, the soul? Again I tell you, they are right behind the door.

Part 1

Chaos:

Complete Disorder —
Confusion — Turmoil

I now realize that our lives are not measured by the calendar as we watch the days, weeks, months and years fly by. But rather are defined by series of events that we live through as we progress on our own life path. These events truly define who we are at our core. Think about your own life. The true significance of what you remember is not usually the time or date when something happened but the emotional result of your experience. The idea that the dates of our birth and death are not as important as the dots in between that defined who we were as a human being makes so much sense to me.

This manuscript was developed over the past decade in my mind and recently committed to paper. I realize now it is an incredibly important dot in my life. As an educator for the past 38 years and especially during the last 16 years as a public school superintendent has not allowed me, for many reasons, to pursue sharing my story until this precise moment. The Universe just has a way of presenting the perfect timing if we listen carefully. I must have known, on some level, that the time would come when I could share my series of experiences or dots. I kept all of the copious notes, cassette tapes and CDs that have been compiled verifying my communication with my loved ones. They have been carefully dated and filed for safekeeping as I moved from place to place. My ultimate purpose is to assure you, the reader, that unconditional love is never ending even through unconditional loss. It transcends all and will remain forever. Losing my son and family members has taught me this law of the universe. I pray that as you read my story it will awaken a part of you and give you both peace and hope to know that the channel of communication is available to you also. You did not lose, on an emotional level, your loved one. They are patiently waiting for you to reconnect with them. Ultimately, my goal is to help others who have experienced the death of a special human being to realize that they are still with them, always and forever. Our loved ones who have moved on want to help us achieve a deeper understanding of the perpetuity of our lives together and help us along our way, especially through our losses. I know this with confidence after experiencing the most difficult loss imaginable —my child.

He Will Take Your Breath Away

May 16, 1999, was an exceptionally beautiful Sunday morning that started out with great promise. It was one of those rare Michigan days with full sun, low humidity and a prediction of a perfect temperature range between 70-75 degrees. The Michigan weather can be challenging, but the change of seasons remarkably wonderful. Michiganders fully appreciate days like this one. It just caused you to want to get outside and do something special to fully enjoy it. I thought a 50-minute drive to Lake Michigan or lunch at one of the unique restaurants along the shoreline would be fun. My husband, 11-year-old son and I were dressed and looking forward to a day together. At 10:00 A.M. the phone rang and it was my 36-year-old son, Ronnie, from Colorado. I could set my watch by his phone call every Sunday morning. He and his wife had twin boys that were weeks away from their third birthday and an older son, nearly seven. We discussed the home they were building *"in God's country"* as he always referred to the small town of Dolores. Ronnie was thrilled about the progress of the home's construction. After having the concrete poured for the foundation, he was so proud to announce to me that the concrete pad was *"only 1/16th of an inch off"* on the entire length of the house. He went on to share the many things he was working on as the general contractor for the house and gave me an update on his businesses as well. He always had so many irons in the fire that I often wondered how he kept it all together. Ronnie was like an energizer bunny that never wore down and didn't seem to need battery replacements; he made his own power. People would come into his stores to talk with him and be around his energy. They inevitably ended up buying something. During one of my visits I sat outside the main entrance of the convenience store just to count the number of customers he had in a 30-minute time frame. It was nonstop. Literally every three minutes or so another person would drive up and make a purchase. He just seemed to have the Midas touch with everything.

He had moved to southern Colorado about ten years earlier to share a business venture with his father. They were going to buy an old convenience/liquor store and make improvements to the structure while building up the business itself. When I first saw the old, dilapidated building I thought a strong wind could blow it over. The scant shelving inside held a few food products that you felt you wanted to check the expiration dates on before purchasing. The well-worn path in the floor tiles indicated the most direct way to get from the cold beverage coolers along the back wall to the cash register. It was quite apparent that liquid refreshments and a small package of assorted snacks were the biggest sellers for the existing store. The overall plan was that his dad, who lived in the area but worked elsewhere, would put up the money to buy the store and Ronnie would work it. When his dad was in town he agreed to help Ronnie, to give him a little break in the grueling schedule. By their projections, the business would be paid off in ten years and they would own it fifty/fifty. The reality was that what started out as a very small, decrepit convenience/liquor store was dramatically transformed. Over the next 10 years it developed into a brand new building three-to-four times larger that also included a popular pizza franchise, a snow mobile dealership, gas station, a separate building for tire purchases and storage, a snow plowing service and a crane service. All of these business ventures were situated close to the beautiful Dolores River and offered many recreational options to the residents of this small town as well as to the large number of hunting and fishing enthusiasts that came to this hunter's paradise on a regular yearly basis. Ronnie's charismatic personality combined with his work ethic and sales ability resulted in significant financial success in all of these endeavors. He had also opened the first tire store in the wealthy town of Telluride, 75 miles away. He always had a vision of what he wanted next to accomplish and lived life at a breakneck pace. To me he epitomized the quote from Yoda, the fictional character in George Lucas's Star Wars movie, *"Do or do not … there is no try."* I tried to encourage him to slow down and enjoy the fruits of his labor but other than a few successful hunting expeditions to Alaska, he worked the stores nonstop. For music enthusiasts among you, the best way to grasp what this guy was all about was to know his preference in music. The group, AC/DC, and their songs, specifically, 'Highway to Hell', 'TNT' and 'High Voltage' best describe him. Of course, I must admit that he said the song that reminded him of me was also by AC/DC, 'She's got balls.' Often, he would take my breath away by his crude remarks about life and thought it quite hilarious. He was not being disrespectful, simply honest and funny. He decided that, in his line of work he could say just about anything he wanted to and get away with it and he did. When he would visit me in Michigan and we would run into someone from the school district he could put on the charm and act so refined in his manners and speech that they would immediately be won over. I used to shake my head later, remembering the chance encounter and think to myself, if you only knew him, really knew him you would be shocked. He was outrageous in so many ways, but serious about his family, his businesses and his responsibilities in life. Ronnie always said that he did not want to be old and infirmed when he died. He was quite serious when he would say that he wanted to die with his boots on. We both believed that every hair on our head was counted and that when your number was up it was up.

As a teenager he always had a job after school. My thought was to keep him busy and out of trouble. His thought was making money and making a deal. Work ethic was something bred into his DNA. Although his touch didn't turn things into gold, it did turn things into money. It was absolutely amazing. He would buy a car that looked like it was duct taped together, make minimal repairs and sell it within a month or so for a nice profit. He could sell, as they say, "bikinis to Eskimos" and then be thanked for the deal!

As I hung up the phone that Sunday morning I remember thinking that there was a palpable difference in him. What was going on? He was calm, gentle and at peace. His voice, softer than usual, combined with the slower rhythm of his speech was a stark difference to his usual fast no-nonsense delivery. Even the words he used seem to be more carefully chosen. I had never heard him sound like this before. It gave me pause and I had the strangest feeling. I flashed back to my office setting. For three consecutive days before this Sunday call as I would answer my office phone I would automatically glance at a picture I had framed of him a few inches away. I seemed compelled to look into his eyes in the picture and the thought just kept coming to me, 'Why are you so sad Ronnie?' I couldn't seem to stop the feelings I had that seemed to be emanating from his eyes in the picture. It seemed crazy. This was the same picture I had looked at for three years and yet over the last few days every time I glanced at it I felt engulfed by such an overwhelming feeling of sadness. As I hung up the phone from his Sunday morning call I just felt something was either dreadfully wrong or at least terribly different in my son's world. What could it be? The significant change in his demeanor that I heard and felt would be confirmed by one of his friends the next day.

Ronnie was a handsome man with light brown hair and a twinkle in his hazel eyes that usually meant he had just done something funny or was planning on it. At 6'2"and 190 pounds, he would walk into a room and with his raunchy sense of humor and one-liners would control it in mere seconds. He always seemed bigger than life not only to me but to most people who knew him. My extended family always referred to him as the "Marlboro Man." He was like a gift that had been purchased that you were trying to neatly place into a gift box and no matter how hard you tried, you couldn't make it fit. He was just more of everything than anyone would have expected. Ronnie would take people's breath away with his comments. Watching their reactions, at first they would seemed puzzled, then slightly offended and would then break out in a hearty laugh at his audacious manner. For example, a very well known and impressive five-star general stopped at his convenience store one day on his drive into Telluride. He asked for something and Ronnie told him to wait a minute he was working with another customer. The general was obviously offended and said to Ronnie, "Do you know who I am?" Nonplussed, Ronnie simply responded, " Well, do you know who I am?" The general, at first taken aback by Ronnie's response, paused to consider it and then ended up breaking out in a big grin and laughed at the encounter.

Ronnie had a passion for hunting, especially big game and was pictured, posthumously, in the Fair Chase magazine published by the Boone and Crockett organization for the Dall sheep that he bagged in the Chugach Mountains of Alaska in 1998. The ram scores were 167-2/8 points. He was absolutely elated! He felt strongly about never wasting or simply killing an animal just for the sake of bragging about it later. He made it a practice to always eat the meat of whatever was killed. I remember opening his freezer once to defrost some meat for dinner. A package was clearly labeled, 'Bear heart.' How in the world do you prepare that, I wondered? I was a city person and this entire environment was challenging to me. I searched in the wild game recipe book for directions on how to cook the bear heart to no avail. My vision of bear meat was that it must be tough and would need to be cooked longer certainly than beef. Not so much! Needless to say that meal was not one of my finest but we ate it anyway.

My mother who loved him deeply said to me once, "I hope you live long enough to raise that child." I replied, "Oh, I will!" He was four years old at the time. As a young child he truly was an "opportunity." He could think of so many things to try — just for the excitement and the thrill of the unknown that I felt I had to be constantly aware and on guard to protect him. When he was five years old we were still living in Michigan and I woke up one Saturday morning about 8 A.M. He was gone! I started to panic. I called his name over and over — inside and outside the house — was he hiding, trying to be funny? I continued to call his name and received no response. Since we lived in a more rural area, there were very few homes nearby. I started to half run down the street to the closest one. Disregarding the hour, I impatiently knocked on the door of our closest neighbors. Yes, they said, Ronnie was there visiting! I apologized to them and on our walk home I asked him why in the world he left the house. Before he could answer I added, "At least you could have written a note!" He looked at me calmly and said, "Mom, I was going to write a note but then I remembered I didn't know how to write." I knew I could not let him get away with anything or it would open the floodgate for his next escapade. My response was simply, "Then you should have drawn me a picture with arrows or something!"

He had a force about him that made those who were faint of heart stop in their tracks. After my divorce from his father and subsequent remarriage we moved to the Denver area. Since we had lived in a much smaller town in Michigan and bus service was provided to the local public school, I was particularly concerned that he be aware and actually practice the rules of safety walking to and from his new elementary school. He was eight years old at the time and together we walked the route to and from school three times on Saturday before school was to begin on Monday. Each time as we crossed Federal Boulevard with the flashing pedestrian light, I pointed out the need to be watchful for oncoming traffic, even if you did have the indicator light to walk. Most importantly, I talked about the issue of stranger danger. I explained to him that this was a huge change for us and we needed to be very careful in this new environment. "Never accept a ride from anyone," I said repeatedly. This was the big city and abiding by the rules of safety was essential. On his first day of school (and my first day teaching in a new school system across the city) I received a call from the Denver Police Department. They had picked him up trying to hitchhike the eight or so blocks to our home. Why? I guess the thrill of the unknown for him was just too much to pass up. He was always willing to try something if it sounded like fun or felt like an adventure. I learned not to ask him why he did something after this experience since his answer was always one of two responses, "I don't know why," or "It sounded like fun."

We were living in the home we purchased in north Denver, next to the Gaslight Theatre. The theatre was in a large corner house that had been refurbished to include seating for 100. It had quite a following with season ticket holders enjoying a new play every two to three months. The owner/director/producer lived in the back of the main floor of the stately building. Theatre patrons entered by going down five steps to the walk-out level and during intermission, were served wine on the patio. It was quite elegant actually. The building was quaint and the setting picturesque with gorgeous rose gardens and a manicured lawn. The only way you would even know the house contained the theatre was a small, rectangular sign discreetly placed in the side yard. Paul, the director was an unusual character. He was a large man with a distinguished British accent that was made more impactful by his habit of enunciating every single syllable with great flair. He was rather aloof and his shock of expertly trimmed white hair indicated a man who was a perfectionist and took everything in life quite seriously. He carried himself with a confidence and dignity befitting a professional. He came to my door soon after we moved in and announced that the previous owners made sure the Alaskan Malamute was inside the house during the evenings the plays were scheduled. This was not presented as a request but more of a formal explanation as to the proper protocol he expected from his new neighbors. No problem, I thought, this was his livelihood and he seemed like a good, if eccentric person. The following spring he came to the front door again but this time asked to speak to Ronnie and me. He explained that he was going to produce a play entitled, Friends and Enemies, which was about a spoiled, rich child and a tutor who had been hired to help him with reading. The story line was that this obstreperous young boy did not see the importance of perfecting his reading skills since his father was rich and could buy anything he needed or wanted. The boy looked at the tutor with a mixture of pity and disdain. It basically consisted of two people in dialogue for one and one-half hours on stage. He wanted Ronnie to audition for the part. Really? This rambunctious boy who lived for football and other rough and tumble elements of life in a play? Refined theatre? I don't think so. Not to be dissuaded, Paul continued by saying that he would pay Ronnie for each performance. Ronnie having absolutely zero interest up to this point looked up at the director and simply said one word. Pay? I tried to explain to Paul that Ronnie had no stage experience and even less interest in pursuing it. Wouldn't he want a young child who absolutely lived to do this sort of thing? I must have been less than convincing because they had both decided by the end of the conversation that this would be a win-win. The deal was sealed. All I could think of was that this was going to be a wild and hairy ride! The next few months involved me helping, actually demanding, that Ronnie memorize his lines and Paul coming to the front door on two different occasions during a break he had called in the rehearsal. Obviously he was at the end of his rope. With raised voice and his white hair flying madly about, he would place his right hand on his heart, as if he was having a heart attack and would seek my immediate assistance with Ronnie's laissez-faire attitude during rehearsal. Eventually, I ended up actually sitting in the first row or two of the theatre, every evening, for the last two weeks of rehearsal. My physical presence being a reminder to Ronnie that he was not suppose to give the director his next line when rehearsing and to pay attention and use emotion in delivering his lines even if this was just a rehearsal. It just about drove Paul crazy. He was 60- plus-years old and his ability to memorize lines was evidently not as good as it used to be. Ronnie thought it was funny to give him his next word or line as Paul would pause momentarily to search his memory for it. Ronnie would watch his face get red as he yelled, "Stop doing that!" Ronnie would also deliver a line in a monotone or too quickly or too slowly, anything to get a rise out of this poor man. At times I thought if Paul makes it through this experience it will be a miracle. Often, before an evening performance, Ronnie would be watching cartoons or still be in his football uniform, with black marks under his eyes at 6:00 P.M. The eye black or smudge that the coach applied to the players seemed to be a symbol of significance and importance to Ronnie as a young player and he left it on frequently during the evenings until reminded to wash it off. As I would feel myself getting nervous about the impending performance I would encourage him to get washed up and dressed since he had to be at the theatre in less than an hour. Completing these tasks, he would saunter, and I do mean saunter, next door in his white pants and navy blue blazer with the gold insignia on the pocket, totally unruffled to arrive just 20 minutes before the play was to start. Every Thursday through Sunday for 32 performances his delivery was perfect. There was never a misstep. He never reviewed his lines or became nervous or uptight before the play would begin. He was so nonchalant about the whole thing that I couldn't believe it. I was beside myself with worry, through each performance. This was a big deal. People paid good money to be entertained. The director's reputation was at stake. But Ronnie never disappointed them. I would go out and sit on my front porch about five minutes before the play was over each evening just waiting and praying that everything turned out all right. I would finally take a deep breath when I heard resounding applause coming from the small theatre. I would give a great sigh of relief and think, Thank God, one more down. At the end of the run the play was judged a huge success and significant accolades were thrown Ronnie's way by the theatre critic for the Denver Post. The extensive review written in the paper mentioned that the young boy (Ronnie) had quite a theatre career ahead of him. Immediately following the last night of the play, a major theatre company in Denver called and asked him to audition for Huckleberry Finn. I couldn't imagine that he would want to do it. We discussed it thoroughly and decided that neither of us wanted to go through this torture again. I called the theatre company back the next day and politely declined. With his earnings from the play he bought a new five-speed bike and put the rest of the money in the bank. At eight-years old he had made quite an impact in the theatre world. I don't believe Paul ever produced another play with a child in it.

Ronnie's excitement of the unknown coupled with his ability to read a situation to determine the point of least resistance made him a force to contend with. When he was in fifth grade he quickly figured out that if he passed the chapter reading tests he would have to move on to harder work. Well, why would a person choose to do that, he thought. Since he preferred action over studying, he decided to work the system. I knew exactly what he was doing and had to meet with a rather indignant teacher and sign a paper assuming responsibility for the decision to move him forward to the more difficult reader without passing the test(s). I could see him in the fifth grade reader as a senior in high school if I didn't intervene. As a teacher I could only imagine my son going through life without the ability to read fluently. He was, however, perfecting his skill of working the system to his advantage. I felt as if a yellow caution light was constantly flashing around him. It signaled me to be observant and prepared at all times and not take my eyes off him for a split second. As an adult he said he could feel my eyes on him from across a room. No kidding! He also used to tell me, *"Mom, don't worry so much."* I felt that one of us needed to be concerned and on alert at all times to make it through life in one piece.

When he was eleven-years old, he and his friends wanted some candy from the grocery store after school. He knew he would be in big trouble with me if he ever stole anything but he wanted to be involved in the thrill of the action. He had some money with him and could have easily paid for the candy — but no — that wouldn't be as much fun. Technically, he felt if he didn't actually steal the candy himself and only drove the get away bike with his friend on the back he really wasn't involved in the theft and consequently wasn't to blame. As a young child, his lack of logic absolutely astounded me at times. Needless to say the police called me, yet again, to discuss his latest escapade.

Throughout the time Ronnie was in school, from Montessori preschool at age four through high-school graduation, I was called at least twice yearly to come into school to discuss a problem. He was not a mean child but just didn't see the rules as something that should be written in stone. He felt that rules should be subject to interpretation or at least up for debate given the unique situations he seem to get himself into. Of course, since he had a hard time passing up a challenge or the thrill of the moment, rules many times just got in the way. I will have to give him this, however, he rarely made the same mistake twice. There was no predictable pattern that could be discerned in his behavior. I realized it was my job as his mother to keep one step ahead of him and I really tried to do so. I never made excuses for him or blamed other students or the school system for his behavior. However, working full time did not allow me to be able to run fast enough or far enough to prevent something from getting out of control and before I knew it, he would be in trouble, yet again. Consequently, I think given his personality and track record, it resulted in the school system expecting him to do something –sometime — someplace that would be against the rules. Knowing this, he never disappointed them!

Over dinner in the fall of his sophomore year in high school he started to complain about a sociology teacher who was spouting off about communism and basically denigrating our system of democracy. Ronnie's ideology was fiercely patriotic and his hero was John Wayne. The saying, "John Wayne, apple pie and motherhood," was something he truly believed in. He was building up a head of steam about this teacher and mentioning him at our evening meals together. I should have intervened at the time. I knew my son, so well, but unfortunately thought it would pass. One afternoon about five days later, the high school principal called me at work. I was now an elementary principal for the school district across the city. He told me they were going to suspend Ronnie. I asked why and he explained that he had gotten into a verbal encounter with his sociology teacher. Basically, as the story came out, as the teacher was going on and on about trying to save enough money to go live in the mountains and leave this terrible capitalist system behind, Ronnie had had it! He stood up and said, *"If you don't like the 'good old US of A' why don't you just leave it?"* The teacher told him to leave the room and Ronnie replied that he wasn't going anywhere, that he belonged there and that the teacher could leave! Unfortunately, the teacher chose to leave the classroom. I asked for a meeting after school of all the people who were concerned and drove to the high school at 4:00 P.M. After a two hour discussion with the principal, assistant principals, the teacher and Ronnie, the teacher admitted he had, in fact, been espousing communism in his class. Since I had heard Ronnie's absolute disdain for this teacher over the dinner table, I figured there must be something to the story. Prior to the meeting I called a few people I knew and did my own investigative work. I discovered that this teacher had a repeated pattern of being moved from one high school to another due to parent complaints regarding the same issue, the promotion of communism. He resigned from teaching the next week.

The high school administration decided to give Ronnie a three-day in school suspension, which I thought was more than fair. Of course, I had to lecture Ronnie when he came home from school that day about respecting adults. But I couldn't help but be a little proud of my son. He was not afraid to stand up for our system of government and potentially made a positive difference in the lives of students in the future who could have been subjected to the brainwashing of this teacher.

The invitations had been sent out in early May and the RSVP's already returned for the major party I had planned to celebrate Ronnie's high school graduation in three weeks. We were all feeling ecstatic. My family was coming from Michigan to celebrate Ronnie's accomplishment! This was going to be a special day. He had made it through high school and with respectable grades, no less! We were so close to the finish line when a problem, once again, surfaced at the high school. He had a large group of friends that he had played football with for years. These students were from all backgrounds and cultures and had a great time together. During their ninth- and tenth-grade years they would come over to the house after their Saturday games and swim in the pool while I made hamburgers and anything else that would fill up eight teenage boys. They all had nicknames for each other relating to their heritage that today you would discipline them for but back then was their way of showing they were part of a tight-knit group that liked to razz each other. No one escaped a 'nickname' and no one seemed to take offense.

On this particular day, Ronnie was walking across the school campus with a few of these friends during a class change when one of the guys said, "*Hey — look at the moon.*" I guess it seemed unusual to him since it was early afternoon. Ronnie, the jokester of the group said, "*You want to see the moon, I'll show you the moon!*" He proceeded to pull down his pants and moon them. Needless to say, when the principal placed this call to me he was justified when he said he had absolutely had it! He explained that they were going to suspend Ronnie to the end of the year and he would not graduate with his class. I was desperate at this point and for the first time in his K-12 school experience I said to the principal, "*Are you sure it was Ronnie?*" He said an art teacher happened to be making a film with her 8mm camera and had it all recorded. I thought to myself, of course, why would I expect Ronnie to do anything that would make it easier for me to negotiate. They graciously gave me the film, which I have still have and will keep for posterity. One day his twins will see it after they graduate from high school. We don't need a repeat performance of that one.

With the phone in one hand and holding the side of my head, elbow on my desk with the other, I was frantically searching for anything I could say that would help the situation. After about thirty seconds I realized that they had nailed him and I knew he deserved it. I just didn't think I deserved it as his mom! He was only three weeks away from graduation, the first major milestone of his life. I wanted to say to the principal, "Give me a break, you try raising him now, I have done my absolute best." I then had a vision of the principal running out of his office, briefcase in hand shouting, "I'm sick and tired of this shit and can't take it anymore!" After briefly entertaining this vision I snapped back to reality. In a very calm, measured response I simply told the principal that if he chose to suspend Ronnie I understood and that they certainly had the right given the circumstance. However, my direct quote was, "*Please understand that although you have to do what you have to do, as a mother I have to do what I have to do. He will be returning to your institution next year and will graduate from your high school.*" Have you ever experienced a pregnant pause? I did that day. There was no response at all, I couldn't even hear breathing on the other end of the phone. Finally I said, "*Are you still there?*" The principal responded rather stoically that he wanted to talk to his assistant principals and would get back to me. Downing three cups of coffee while waiting nervously for the principal to respond he called back. The forty-five minutes that had elapsed between calls felt like a lifetime. He said that they had decided to call it a senior prank and would give Ronnie a three-week, in-school suspension in the media center. He would be allowed to graduate with his class if there were no other incidences. Trying to simultaneously mask my conflicted feelings of total embarrassment and jubilation, I simply commented to the principal that I felt that he had made a very wise decision. What I really wanted to do was fall on my knees in front of him and first thank him and then apologize profusely for the problems that Ronnie had been involved in over the past four years of high school. School staff should not be expected to take that kind of ongoing misbehavior. I knew in every bone in my body that he deserved the punishment that the principal had originally planned to give him. But I was at the end of my rope and just wanted this part to be over. As a mother I was desperate at this point and threw my "principal hat" aside and went for broke. Ronnie graduated in May of that year and I gave a great sigh of relief. We had made it this far.

I knew from his personality that he had to be totally invested in whatever he wanted to do. I never paid for his car, insurance or even gas. Knowing that if I did he would not feel the consequences of his decisions. Nonetheless, after his second vehicle was bought and sold he could finally afford a used Jeep, a vehicle he had wanted for some time since it was so 'cool.' He drove in the driveway and yelled to me, *"Mom, come see — ROCK AND ROLL!!"* I remember thinking, *"Oh God, here we go again!"* I must admit it was a sharp looking burnt orange color with a rag top. I was concerned that the soft top would not be safe but he pointed out the roll bars overhead that would help to protect him in case of a roll over. He was nearly 18 years old and had owned the jeep about four months when he drag raced a car down Colfax Avenue, a major thoroughfare in Denver. He didn't know the other driver who revved his engine at a stop signal but simply revved his engine in return and yelled, *"You want a piece of me?"* A race ensued. I received a call just before midnight from the Jefferson County Police Department. Of course, midnight was his curfew on week-ends, and I was wondering where he was anyway. They said I needed to come down to get him. Before bringing him out to me the young police officer said with a small smile on his face, *"That was one of the best races I've ever seen! He could have accrued twenty-two points against his license. But he was very respectful when we finally stopped him."* The officer went on to explain that the other boy did not follow their directives to "hit the ground and spread 'em." However, Ronnie was extremely careful to treat the officers with respect. My son always knew when to hold and when to fold, to paraphrase a line from the famous song by Kenny Rogers. I took the keys to his jeep from the officer and locked them in my safety deposit vault for three months. For the entire week after the race when I talked to Ronnie I referred to him as, "killer." I know this sounds terribly harsh but I had to get his attention! He really could have killed himself and others in this latest fiasco. After a week he asked me to please stop referring to him that way and I agreed. I made him promise in return that he would never drag race like that again! I just found in raising him, I had to be more dramatic than he was to get his attention at times.

Soon after graduation from high school I had made arrangements for us to visit a college in Colorado. The campus was nestled in the beautiful Rocky Mountains. It was such a serene setting surrounded by huge Ponderosa pine trees and a sprawling campus of green mountain grass. You could just imagine the wildlife that would wander around after dusk when the students had finished their classes for the day. I knew he would love the setting, in was right up his alley, the studying part, I was not sure of. But I thought he would be safe there and able to grow up a bit while expanding his world and deciding what he wanted to pursue in life. Our visit took place in late May since it had taken me months - actually years- to convince Ronnie that it would do him good to go to college —or at least to visit the campus and see how he felt about the idea. Although he was not at all excited about the prospect, I thought once he became acclimated to college life he would see the benefits and begin to enjoy it. The staff member who showed us around the campus was actually the football coach. He wanted Ronnie to play for the college. As he took us around I kept watching Ronnie for the least bit of excitement. Nothing. They set out a delicious lunch for us in the faculty lounge, which Ronnie hardly touched. We had met with the registrar who explained that they even gave PE credit for down hill skiing. Seriously, I thought how good could it get. He loved to ski. He could even bring his jeep to school as a freshman! The last thing we visited was the dorms. As we peered into an empty fourteen-by-fourteen-foot room, there were twin beds on opposite walls with a desk at each end. Ronnie looked at me and said, *"Where would I put my bedroom suite?"* I knew this wasn't a good sign but I gently explained that he wouldn't have to worry about moving it here, since there wasn't space for it and all the students slept in individual twin beds in the dorms. It would remain safe at home when he came to visit. He looked cautiously at the room again and said, "*There are two beds in here. Do you mean there are two people in this one room?*" I said, yes but the good news was that many students studied in the larger group areas, the library or cafeteria. I added that students spend a lot of time away from their rooms. I could tell by his reaction that he wasn't buying it and was not the least bit excited by the prospect of college. He was quiet for most of the three-hour drive back to Denver. About 30 minutes from the city he just calmly announced that he wasn't ready to leave home. I tried to encourage him to give college a chance and if he didn't like it, we would find something else. I explained to him that I left home at seventeen-years old and he was eighteen. I even threw in that he wouldn't have me watching his every move. I tried everything I could think of to motivate him to attend college, all to no avail. He had made up his mind during the spring of his senior year that he didn't want to go to college and that was it. He wasn't going. He would get a full time job and let life unfold.

Even though he didn't attend college, within one year of graduation from high school, at age nineteen, he became the manager of a tire store. He was making seventy percent of what I was making as an elementary principal. In fact, he was so hardworking and successful that the company, which was a national chain, moved him to three different locations in the Denver area over a three year period to increase the sales of each store he was managing. He bought his first house at age twenty-one because, as he explained to me, he needed the tax write off! Interestingly, however, when his younger brother at age eleven told Ronnie one day that he thought he would take a year off between high school graduation and college, Ronnie absolutely flipped out and told him he would do no such thing! He also made sure that when their twins were born each of the boys had a college fund established. Even though college wasn't for him he realized, in retrospect, how hard he had to work and he wanted more for them. He worked twelve to fourteen plus hours every day to achieve what he wanted in life. At thirty-six-years old he often looked so exhausted that I felt sorry for him. He never stopped pushing himself and as his responsibilities grew he just seemed to make himself work harder and faster.

Trust me these examples merely skim the surface of my son's life. There are so many more that I could have included in this book that it would have ended up to be 800 pages. But I wanted you to have an understanding of his multifaceted personality and the strong person that he was, and still is, in my thinking. A risk taker, great debater, a daredevil, a "change the rules if they don't make sense" kind of guy on one hand and a loving, caring, extremely hard-working son and great father and husband on the other. He would go out of his way to help someone without discussion or fanfare. He really was one-of-a-kind.

Ronnie had an especially tender side toward his elders whether family or acquaintances and would always lend a hand to help them out. There was an older man on a fixed income in Dolores that regularly stopped for gas at his station. Although it was self-serve, Ronnie always ran out to pump his gas and while doing so would tell the man that he had a pizza that had been sitting over fifteen minutes and needed to be thrown away according to the rules of the pizza franchise. Would he just please do Ronnie a favor and take it for free? He knew the man had very little to live on but was careful to say things in a way that kept the man's pride in tact. I would bet that man had two meals every week from those pizzas.

The Accident that Devastated Our High School

I had been working as a superintendent in a suburban school district in Michigan since 1991 and it was common to have parents or community members call my home for issues that seemed critically important to them. It was part of the 24/7 expectation that encompasses most superintendents' contracts. Parents need help and support on their own time frame. They may be on their last nerve and near a breaking point over a weekend. Many times they just can't wait for the next workday to make contact. I chose to live within the district that I served and encouraged an open door policy. Consequently, I had received calls at 2:00 A.M. asking me if we were going to have a snow day, calls to find out when school would start for the year, calls complaining about a teacher or administrator and, of course, calls regarding discipline issues involving their sons or daughters. Everyone has his own definition of emergency. When the calls came I felt it was just part of my job and I took them seriously.

Instantly, after hanging up from the phone call from Ronnie on the

Sunday morning, the phone rang a second time. It was a parent asking me to help contact another parent who was away on a trip to Detroit with some students. This parent was crying and told me that there had been a terrible car accident involving five of our soon-to-graduate senior boys. It had happened a few hours earlier in another town. They were hit or "T-boned" by another vehicle. The parent went on to say that they could not reach the mother who was out of town to inform her about the accident and tell her that her son had been one of the boys who was injured. Contact was made then through a series of calls and I left to go directly to the hospital.

Once I arrived at the hospital, a priest from our local church met me outside at the emergency drop off curb and asked me to meet with him, a doctor and the parents of one of the students who had been killed in the accident. I was dumbstruck. I had only been told that there had been a 'terrible accident.' Until that moment I hadn't realized any of our boys had actually lost their lives. I kept thinking about the parents who were driving down to the hospital and would hear the news. At least for the moment they thought their son was still alive. Once they were told the tragic news there was no going back. Oh, God, what could I do to help? What could I say? Since they were parishioners at the local Catholic Church someone thought to call their priest. Thankfully, he would be there with me to meet with them and offer comfort. The minutes were ticking away and all the time we were standing at the curb of the emergency entrance I kept thinking — take your time — there is no hurry to hear the words that will change your lives forever.

Less than ten minutes later they arrived. When the mother saw me she said, "Dr. Leiker, why are you here?" I didn't know how to respond so instead mumbled something I'm sure, in retrospect, was incoherent. We were all escorted to a small room, which seemed more like a triangular closet with just enough space for three or four people. The air felt lifeless. It was a place that you just naturally wanted to run from. You could feel the pain radiating out of the walls. The windowless room had nothing in it other than a very small couch and two straight-back chairs. I didn't know how the terrible news would be given to the parents. I looked around for water, coffee or tissues, anything that could be needed. Nothing. I had never been in a face-to-face situation like this before where parents were involved. I was so shocked by what I felt was lack of anticipation of need. I knew the mother since she had worked for us in the school district. I prayed for the strength to help these parents who would soon be receiving the news about their son that would rock their world so completely that life would never be the same again.

The father chose to stand rather than take the seat that was available. Strange as it may seem, it only took about one or two minutes for the doctor to tell these parents that their son was dead. There was no leading up to this bombshell, no empathy exhibited, just the message. A heavy silence engulfed the room. The mother after hearing the news and trying to process it, leaned over and put her head on my shoulder and began to sob quietly.

I wanted to scream at the doctor! Is this the best you can do? This isn't a statistic or a medical procedure. This is a family who has just been informed that their son was killed. Can't you show some emotion, do something to help them? The father was standing near the doorway trying to keep it together and appeared both angry and shocked as he heard the information. I thought his legs were going to give out from under him. I remember saying to myself, this family has just experienced the greatest loss possible — their son, there but by the grace of God, go I.

I stayed at the hospital for the rest of the day. Another student from the accident was in critical condition and in surgery; the third student was being evaluated and had serious head injuries. Would surgery be necessary? No one knew at this point. The fourth student had minor injuries. He had been in the passenger seat of the car.

The story unfolded during the day. It seemed the boys, having reached the legal gambling age of eighteen were feeling, as seniors often do, that the world was their oyster and they were invincible. They had decided to drive to a gambling casino out of town and left around 11:00 P.M. Saturday evening. They were going to graduate in a few weeks and were just trying to experience a little of what life had to offer before going their own separate ways after graduation. They were apparently hurrying back to the city the next morning since some were planning to attend church services. They were obviously exhausted from being up all night and did not see the car approaching the intersection. As their car was hit, the driver and passenger were hurt but not fatally injured. Of the three boys in the back seat, the two boys, each by a window, were killed and the other boy sitting between them was critically injured. It was so fast, so unexpected, so very tragic. If only we could have moved the hands of the clock back slightly, even two or three seconds, and given the boys the gift of time to survive.

Students have an effective and efficient communication system so, by now, the students from the school district had heard about the accident and many of them came to the hospital to support each other and the families. Everywhere you looked more students appeared throughout the day. They were sitting in chairs, on the floors and in different waiting rooms of the hospital. The nurses and other hospital support staff were outstanding. They did not try to limit the incredible number of students coming into the waiting rooms and just seemed to understand their need to be together. All of the high school administrative staff and many of the instructional staff members came to the hospital during the day as well. It seemed as if we were living out a movie scene in hopes that someone would yell, "Cut" and everything would go back to normal.

It is hard to explain the reactions of large groups of students to someone who has not worked in the field. When a life trauma happens, students want and need to be around each other. They need the support and physical proximity of their friends to help them cope with the tragedy. They are trying desperately to process information and events that are new to them and completely out of their comfort zone. They need to cry together. Share stories of the students involved. They need the hugs from their peers to give them strength. They look to the adults for answers. When there are no answers forthcoming to explain the terrible events and the probable outcomes they feel vulnerable and frightened. In essence, they look to the adults to "fix it." Death, however, doesn't get fixed.

In their minds they are trying to understand but it just doesn't make any sense. Teenagers usually think they will live forever. Particularly in the video game era that these students were raised in, the hero can be killed and then magically reappear again in the next sequel. Students don't think about death unless they have lost someone close to them. After all, life has just begun for them. Yet, here were between ninety and 110 teenagers at any given time on different floors, using the elevators to check for updates on each of the three boys who were still alive. We waited and many of us prayed silently as the minutes ticked away into hours. We were struggling with the greatest challenge in life — to accept the helplessness involved in understanding and accepting the finality of death and the uncertainty of the future. The students were trying to process that two of their peers were dead and two more in serious to critical condition. What was going on in the operating rooms? Would the boys be alive tomorrow? The fact that one of the students had miraculously survived with minor injuries was greeted with gratefulness but overshadowed by the weight of the rest of the overwhelming tragedy. You could see the uncertainty in the eyes of students and staff who were also struggling with their own mortality. This was the tragic part of life — of growing up — and learning that loss is something that we are unprepared for but must, nonetheless, accept. There is a beginning and ending to all things physical.

Around 4:00 P.M. after surgery was completed on one of the boys and the other two appeared stable, the high school principal and I decided to leave and drive to the home of the fifth student who was in the car but never made it to the hospital. He had been killed instantly in the accident and his parents had been notified much earlier that morning. As we drove to their home about twenty-five minutes away, I kept thinking to myself how could this have happened? Yesterday, at this very moment, these boys were still alive and planning their weekend, their lives. As we stepped into the home I remember it being so very quiet. The parents and their daughter were sitting at the kitchen table and appeared, naturally, to be in shock. They explained that family, friends and neighbors had come in and out during the day to offer condolences, bring food that appeared untouched or just stopped by to give them a hug. We sat with them and talked quietly. What do you say? " I'm so sorry," of course and then what? You listen. It is the greatest gift you can give to someone who is in grief. The parents kept talking about their son as a young child, then as a young man who was ready to graduate. We continued to listen. They talked about the graduation party that would need to be cancelled, the grandchildren they would never see. It was heartbreaking. After an hour or so we hugged them and told them we would see them in the next few days. None of us mention the word funeral but we all knew what was left unsaid.

The parents of the two boys who were killed would have to put their mourning on hold and make arrangements instead to bury them. Knowing that their sons would not be graduating from high school in three weeks, even as their caps and gowns hung in anticipation in their closets, was a devastating blow and cruel twist of fate. They had made it to the finish line of their high school experience and been swept away, ironically, at the very end of it. Sadly, their future dorm rooms at college, which signified their future hopes and dreams, would have to be relinquished. Tragically, these parents would never be able to hug these children again or hear their sons' voices or laugh with them. They would not be able to watch them achieve their dreams. The immensity of their loss elicited a pain so intense that it was indescribable. The atmosphere in their home was filled with a grief so deep it seemed to be absorbed into your very being. Tomorrow would be another day but not a typical day for the families of the boys who had been killed. They would be facing the decisions about funeral services, burial sites, finding pictures to display of their sons' lives from birth to age eighteen. Their senior portraits, intended for display at their graduation parties would be used, instead, at the entryway of the funeral homes. These parents would be expected to function both mentally and physically and make all the decisions necessary to bury their beloved sons. In the meantime no bandage existed that could relieve their bleeding hearts.

The principal had called an emergency meeting of the counseling staff, social worker and other key people and staff from the high school for 7:00 P.M. that night to prepare for the next day. The entire student body would be coming back tomorrow from the weekend to face the reality of death. Since the students in the accident had, for the most part, been in the district their entire K-12 school life, most all of the other students knew them or knew of them even though it was a large, 1,800 student, 10-12-grade high school. These boys had been a part of the lives of so many other students. In addition to sharing academic classes the students knew each other from school trips, sports teams, music groups and end-of-year or summer activities. They had made so many friends that the entire student body would feel the effect of their passing. They were an integral part of this active, growing community.

I went home for thirty minutes to prepare some dinner for my family and then hurried back to the high school to be a part of the crisis meeting. The school administrators and staff did an incredible job getting ready for the next day. Plans to help students and staff cope with the news included a discussion from the social worker and counselors of possible reactions to anticipate the next day. There would be crying, possible hysteria, even students who might laugh nervously or joke about the accident to hide their feelings of insecurity and fear. Some teachers might not be able to teach, especially if they had any of the students who were involved in the accident in their classrooms.

Other concerns surfaced about staff. How could the team be prepared to assist any staff member who might have an especially difficult time coping the next day? Did anyone know of any staff member who had recently experienced a loss in their own life? If so, their feelings would still be particularly sensitive. How would they cover the classes of any teachers who might have to leave during the day and just go home if the stress became too great? Almost on cue as if to demonstrate, one of the teachers actually had to leave the crisis meeting that evening as she became overwhelmed with her personal feelings. Staff members in this large high school had experienced loss from death, divorce, illness and other things. They were a microcosm of society. How many of them would actually be able to make it through the incredibly difficult days and weeks ahead and put their own feelings on hold? To ask them to do this, whether they were professionals or support staff, is an immense thing to do. Yet we had no other option. Life would go forth tomorrow and everyone needed to be ready to pick up the pieces.

The burden of responsibility was on the staff and administrators as never before. Would they be able to do it all and remain a model of calm and supportive adults to help the students' better cope with this life-changing event? The truth of the matter is that we have no choice as educators but to respond in a way that is sympathetic and concerned yet calm and controlled. The other equally powerful truth is that as educators we are people, human beings first, and educators second. Yet superhuman expectancies are needed in life altering moments such as those before us. It is something you are never trained for in your college curriculum but must learn as on-the-job-training.

I have watched others under conditions similar to what was before us manifest their stress uniquely and, at times, unpredictably. There seems to be no cookie cutter way to handle the pressure involved in uncertainty and loss. Consequently, there is no formula or template to use to help them. The various responses and reactions are as individually unique as the people involved. It is not uncommon to see people start to organize things in their environment in an attempt to gain some sense of personal control. I remember starting to clean and organize a kitchen cupboard after the doctor told me that a family member would probably not make it through surgery. I needed to do something to keep my hands occupied, my world intact as it seemed to spin out of control. Other people may want to read to gain information to help them better process the situation and what is happening to them. Many people just need to talk with someone as a way to work through the stages of grief. They may even need to continually repeat the same stories of the lives of their loved one as a step in accepting the tragedy before them. They are not looking for answers but simply need to use their voice as a salve to heal their internal wounds. Still others retreat unto themselves. The immensity of their grief is too great for them to even communicate with family members or colleagues and be able to continue to function. It seems their brains are on overload and they can only do one thing at a time. As administrators you simply do not know until the school doors open the next day which staff will be able to remain standing through the agony and near hysteria of many of the students. There is no greater challenge to staff than times like the one that was before us. The principal and his team were incredible. I thank them now, as I did then, for their professionalism.

Other areas of concern involving both students and staff surfaced. For instance, how should the empty seats that these students normally occupied be handled? The emptiness would be a stark visual reminder that a peer was missing. However, to remove the empty seats would seem disrespectful, a closure too soon in coming. Should teaching go on as usual or should a discussion of the accident and the loss of lives be undertaken by each teacher with their classes? Would all of the nearly ninety teachers in the 10-12 building as well as the thirty teachers in the ninth-grade building next door be able to handle a discussion of this sort themselves? These were subject matter specialists not counselors by training. There were so many questions, concerns and possible results to consider. The possibilities were truly endless. Having bottles of water, juice, snacks and tissues available in the hallways and classrooms were covered. They may seem like small things but are invaluable to consider and plan for in times of heightened stress. We could not afford to have a sugar drop or dehydration of a student take place. That would add to the overwhelming fear the students were already facing.

This was a very close-knit community. It was not uncommon for students to graduate from college, marry and return to this community to raise their children in our schools. Since there was no official downtown area in our suburb, the school buildings, particularly the high school was looked upon as the center of the community. Many of the residents knew each other or at least knew of the students or families involved in the horrific accident. The rest of our parents would want to know of the funeral arrangements and revised schedule of classes for the week. They might need to have a place to talk with other parents to console themselves. Our job was to infuse a sense of security that everything was under control in the school setting. Parents would then feel empowered to assure their own children that they were safe and the sun would come up tomorrow even if the clouds gathered in the sky as if to mourn the passing of our kids.

It was expected that some parents would naturally want to come to school to discuss what happened. Regardless of what the local news was reporting, some parents needed to hear it directly from someone in the school setting that they knew and trusted. We would need a plan to have someone available for these parents as well. Of course, a letter needed to be drafted to go home to all parents the next day explaining the life changing events and revised schedule for the week. The list went on and on with individual staff members jumping in and offering to take on particular responsibilities. They thought of so many things to help students, other staff members and parents get through the next few days. The meeting was all consuming, as it should be.

The issue of calling school off to attend the funerals was an issue to be contended with. When the State Department issues a mandate that the school year will consist of 180 days or 1,080 hours, as they did in 1999, they simply can't foresee events of this magnitude. But what administrator with a good conscience would deny students from attending the funerals of fellow students? Do we call school off for the days of the funerals and risk losing the per diem funding from the state or leave the decision to the students and parents themselves? We needed to find a way to allow their absences as "excused" whether they actually were close friends with the boys who died or mere acquaintances. Some students might not actually attend the funerals and use the time to do other things. That was a risk we needed to be able to take. State funding be damned.

The stages of loss were discussed very briefly. But how can a person truly understand these stages in five minutes coverage? It becomes dreadfully clear that a lack of understanding about these stages makes the situation we were in that much more dire. Elisabeth Kübler-Ross has said that if life is truly a classroom, then loss is a major part of the curriculum. However, it is something we don't teach in schools and something that most families don't even want to talk about. Yet, here we were at a crossroads. How do you console and support students when they are pleading for help in understanding their own feelings of fear and abandonment? Some students wanted an explanation of death, what happens exactly and what is next? When many adults in their lives have chosen to avoid the topic it makes responding to these students that much more difficult. Making their concerns even more complex was the fact that there were so many different religious philosophies in this diverse community how could you possibly say enough to include all of them. As humans some of us seem driven to learn more about our existence, to probe further into the possibilities of the Universe. However as public school educators this area must be dealt with so carefully and with the inclusion not exclusion of the various belief systems. Even if the world has been unable to handle the differences that exist in belief systems, students, at times like these, wanted and needed answers. The clergy in this community called and offered assistance to anyone in need.

A school is truly like a family. If one person hurts, we all seem to hurt. In addition to the students in this tenth through twelfth-grade building there were another 600 plus students in the ninth-grade building across the parking lot. Well over 2,400 students would be returning in a matter of eleven hours. Each would be trying to find a way to cope and accept the news that two of their peers were dead and three more of their friends in the hospital, two still in critical condition. Many of the students who were in the accident had younger or older siblings that were well known. The web of loss and grief just kept growing exponentially.

The staff of any middle or high school learns to be prepared for an innumerable number of possible reactions from students given the emotional rollercoaster of young adolescents who often don't think before they 'do.' I cannot describe how tragic and emotionally draining the day had been. We had lost students to disease, accidents and even a suicide during my first eight years in the district. But the magnitude of five students about to graduate all involved in an accident at the same time was overwhelming. Tomorrow was coming and I needed to be prepared for what — I wasn't sure. I just knew it would be one of the toughest days of my life.

While driving the ten minutes to get to my home after the meeting, my mind was trying to grapple with the events of the day. I kept seeing the faces of the parents who had lost their boys. After eighteen years of trying their best to guide and raise their sons, it was over. Vanished in the night like a dream that flits in and out of consciousness. What would they do now? How would they cope? Their words echoed in my head. Why, why, why? None of us could fully comprehend what had happened. Their sons were gone. I couldn't help them. I couldn't take their pain away. I thought I was a strong leader but felt helpless in the wake of this terrible tragedy. Little did I know that within fifteen minutes I would join the ranks of these parents and be brought to my knees as a mother.

The Call that Night that Changed My Life Forever

Arriving home from the crisis meeting I told my husband and son that I was physically and emotionally spent and went directly to the bedroom to get ready for bed. Although I hadn't eaten anything since the night before, I was beyond trying at this point. The day had been indescribably difficult and so very exhausting. Tomorrow was coming and we all had more questions than answers. The phone rang, and it was my daughter-in-law. She told my husband that she needed to talk to me. He explained to her that I had a very difficult day and now wasn't a good time to talk. It was then that she spoke the words that altered my life forever. "I need to talk to her, Ronnie is dead!" I remember where I was standing in the bedroom when my husband said the words to me, "Gina needs to talk to you." I responded, "Not tonight, I can't even think." He repeated, "She needs to talk to you," and added, "Ronnie is dead."

I remember yelling at him, "Take it back — it's not true" — as he handed me the phone. Somehow I managed to hear Gina's voice over the phone although it sounded like she was in a tunnel. I wanted to drop the phone and simply start running. I wanted to escape from the news and make it disappear into thin air. I struggled to process the words as she said them to me. I just kept thinking as she talked, no, it isn't true, it can't be true. How she had the strength to tell me herself I'll never know. She had been training paramedics and knew a great deal about emergency situations. She said they had let her work on him for forty-five minutes and then ceased efforts. A helicopter had landed so that the crew could assist. She felt that they knew it was hopeless but since they knew her, they gave her the time she felt she needed to try to revive him. He never regained consciousness. He had been the love of her life and she tried to assure me on the phone that she had tried everything to save him. I knew that if anyone could have saved him, she could.

Gina wanted to explain exactly what happened. He had gone out to the building site of their new home that afternoon and wanted to tamp the ground in the garage area so it would be totally prepped when the crew came the next day to pour the concrete for the garage floor. He was on a front loader that he had borrowed from a friend. Since it was an old model it did not have a guard on it to protect the operator. Later we found out that in addition to the lack of a protective guard on the machine, the owner had made some type of modification to it which nullified any responsibility on the part of the manufacture. Ronnie had seen something in the dirt and leaned over the front loader to pick it up. As his left knee bumped the lever connected to the bucket, his six-foot, two-inch frame and 190-pound body was no match as the bucket came crashing down. The cross bar on the bucket frame pinned him down over the front of the machine as the pressure from his knee continued to keep the deadly force of the machine inching out every last bit of air in his lungs. His chest was crushed and his spleen ruptured. Ironically, as he stated to me months earlier, he died with his boots on.

With the three kids in the car, Gina stopped at her dad's house near the property on her way to the building site. She was trying to find out why he hadn't come home for dinner. There was Ronnie pinned down by the machine and it was still running. Regardless of his size and physical strength he was no match for the front loader. The machine won. In an instant, life changed for all of us. I had lost my son, my precious first born. Gina lost the love of her life. The boys had lost their doting father. Ronnie's children would never again see his broad grin at the end of a workday, feel the warmth of his heart as he hugged them as he walked through the door. There would never be another Father's Day to celebrate with him.

To this day, I believe fears of abandonment and loss can remain so deeply seated in the recesses in minds of young children who experience a tragedy of this type that my heart aches for them. When children are so young they cannot comprehend the finality of life, as we know it. Their confusion and inability to discuss it in depth with others traps them in a place of grief and uncertainty. Especially in young children, the lack of mere words and concepts prevent them from understanding and processing their grief. Their lives will never be the same. The grief remains buried in their minds until later in life when it eventually surfaces. Sometimes with an intensity that even surprises them. Dr. Kübler-Ross talks a great deal about early memories that may need to be processed through later in life in order to heal the anger and grief that is carried in the subconscious.

After the phone call from Gina, I just kept repeating Ronnie's name. Nothing else, no other words would come out of my mouth, I just remember crying, "Ronnie, Ronnie, Ronnie." My son couldn't be dead. No, this was a bad dream. The day had been so difficult, so emotional this wasn't — couldn't — be happening! I kept thinking, I'll wake up and it won't be true. The trouble was, however, I was awake and it was true.

Over the years, I have observed that certain words can be read a million times and the actual meaning or intent understood on a more superficial level until you have actually experienced the perfect embodiment of the definition. Then it truly stops you in your tracks and the real meaning hits you like a ton of bricks. Such was the word "surreal" for me that day. Even today when I hear or read that word I understand it in the depth of my soul. Reflecting back on May 16, 1999, it was as if the world had stopped and so much was happening that my mind was in a continuous feedback loop between fact and denial. This could not have happened! It was beyond my comprehension. My mind said one thing, my heart another.

In the movie, *Steel Magnolias,* Sally Field's character said at her daughter's gravesite, "I know my daughter is in a better place and I should feel good about that, but I just wish someone would tell that to my heart." She was nearly hysterical and yet soon after began to laugh about her hair. It sounds bizarre to pair these two emotions doesn't it? That scene, even when I watch the movie to this day just takes my breath away. I now understand completely what she was saying. It was written and acted so perfectly. A parent who loses their child or close loved one can relate to the depth of her grief and conflicting emotions in the movie. It seems oddly inappropriate that the people in our world continue on with their daily lives. You want to yell at them and say, "Stop, don't you understand my son is dead!" Of course they do not. They are continuing on with their daily lives not out of disrespect but from survival, expectation and responsibility.

Our eleven-year old son ran into the bedroom when he heard me scream as I was told the news and kept saying, "Mom, remember how we believe." Over and over he kept saying the same sentence. The trouble was I couldn't process anything I heard. My brain had shut down. I remember the school board president, my administrative assistant, best friend, sister and nieces coming to the house within what seemed like moments of hearing the news. Others continued to arrive over the next few hours. Plane reservations were made, clothes packed and repacked as I struggled to find something to do physically while my mind, my thought process was on hold. Since I was unable to sleep my sister stayed up with me all night and listened to me as I kept trying to process what had happened. At one point I remember saying, *"Phyllis, Ronnie didn't die,* (I couldn't process that word in my mind or heart) *but he was killed in an accident."* This distinction of words, again, might sound strange and I suppose it is in retrospect. Knowing my son, however, and his "living on the edge" type of personality, I seemed to be able to verbalize the word "killed." During the night I thought it had begun to sink into my brain and I was beginning to accept what had happened to my son. I was quite wrong.

Among the many ironies of this tragedy was that Ronnie was certified as a crane operator and had worked with heavy equipment for a few years in the Denver metro area before moving to southern Colorado. He was not a novice in the field of powerful machinery. Unfortunately, this machine was quite old and the company has since changed the design to protect the operators against this type of injury. But for us it was too late. He was gone.

Since that day any mention in the newspaper or on TV of someone being killed on a piece of machinery jumps out at me. I realize the companies that manufacture the machinery itself cannot protect everyone in every circumstance. But I would like to meet with the designers to say, let me show you my broken heart. This is another phrase I feel that is known in the mind, but not experienced by the heart until a tragedy of this magnitude happens.

In the area of my heart I actually had a pain, a dull, heaviness that would not go away. I have said my son's death left a hole in my heart or maybe it's more like scar tissue on the heart after a heart attack. You instinctively know it will never be the same again but you try to put one foot in front of the other and continue on. But, the heaviness remains. I can't imagine how the engineers who design equipment that fails must feel when their design ends up causing someone to lose their life.

It is so terribly sad that the understanding of the words, "broken heart" is often lost by companies as they look at the bottom line profit margin. Their engineering diligence or lack thereof, however, can mean the difference between a life well lived or a life cut short. It can mean the difference between young children who have a daddy to look up to and be supported by or a mere distant memory that will fade over time unless the family works to keep it alive.

I realize we are a litigious society and frequently hear of frivolous lawsuits. I have always lived by the rule that to work for a living is much more beneficial to self and society that to sue someone or some entity. But what is equally shocking to me is that a company will do everything in their power with their legal teams to "prove" it was not the fault of their equipment, even after they have made design changes for greater safety due to previous deaths in similar circumstances.

Is it possible in our world to ever create a "Sorry from Our Heart Compensation Fund" to the spouse and children involved in this type of loss? Not admitting error, necessarily, but showing remorse and recognition of the pain that has been created. Can you just imagine the image and reputation this corporate mentality would elicit? Slogans such as, The Company that Really Cares, or We Walk Our Talk/Your Safety IS the Issue would actually mean something! When a life is cut short corporate respect and remorse could make such a difference. Certainly, their advertising, insurance and legal budgets could be reduced significantly if structured correctly. A company would only have to show up once, to a grieving family, with a check in hand and say, we may not be responsible but "we are sorry from our heart," for the reputation of such a company in our internet driven world to blast their positive image as a company into the homes and businesses of millions of people around the world. I refuse to believe that this approach is too naïve to take seed. One individual can change the world given a positive intention. We are better than we often demonstrate. A company, sometime, someplace will say — let's give it a try. Life will be better for it.

I can't change the type of corporate mentality that presently exists but I just wonder how the human beings behind the corporate walls would handle the loss of their child if it happened on a piece of equipment they designed. I would never wish it on them but as Ronnie used to say, "what goes around comes around." It may not be the same lesson but a lesson, nonetheless, will be presented to them, which will stop them in their tracks until it is learned. After all, the law of cause and effect is alive and well and living on planet Earth!

Since we were working in Michigan at the time, it took seven or eight hours to get to southern Colorado. Three airports and three planes later we arrived in Cortez, Colorado. I remember as we flew tears just kept running down my cheeks. I could not stop them. Even when I couldn't think and just felt like I was in the ozone, the tears were there. When we arrived in Cortez, we went directly to the funeral home.

I asked the funeral director, nicely, to see my son then had to demand to see him. Sometime during the middle of the night when I was using the word "killed" to my sister and the next few hours I was back in the denial stage again. I was certain I could make him get up and go back to business as usual. Ronnie always felt I could accomplish anything I put my mind to and I thought the same of him. Well, my heart said I wanted him to wake up and stop this. But my heart and my head were not in sync.

I realize, now, that I was caught between the denial and anger stages of loss. The director came back to me three times with a different excuse. He said, "He isn't cleaned up, he isn't ready, his body is cold." The last statement put me over the top. I looked at him with a fury not altogether controlled and said, "Don't you realize a child is never cold to their mother?" Finally he tried one more approach and said, " He's not even here, he's across the street." They obviously had a building across the street to store the bodies (a word neither the director nor myself used at that time). That thought can put you over the edge as well! I tried to control myself but lost any semblance of patience or dignity I had. I felt I was losing ground fast with the director and became so desperate that I just shouted, "Go get my son! And for God's sake don't wheel him across the street."

That funeral director seemed to literally recoil from me. Granted, it was a small town, small funeral home, small everything it seemed and I'm sure I came across much too assertive. I've heard of doctors that do not have any bedside manner but can you imagine a funeral director responding this way? Of course, I can't imagine what type of personality it would take to be able to do that job for a living. I certainly couldn't do it. And we will all need them sooner or later. It would take both art and skill to be able to judge the unique emotional needs of the family members they work with and try to respond accordingly. If your job is working with people and their losses, day after day, with their accompanying denial, grief and anger it could cause you to slip, occasionally, and not say the most appropriate thing. Empathy, however, cannot be feigned. After what seemed like a lifetime of waiting, he came out and told me Ronnie was in the next room. I appreciated my husband saying he and our eleven-year old son would wait for me so I could go in first to see Ronnie.

As I walked up to the gurney he was on I thought he looked like he was sleeping. He was dressed in his familiar jeans and a stripped shirt that I had bought him years before. His sleeves were rolled up as usual. There was a little blood near his nose and his left eyelid was slightly bruised but other than that he actually looked at peace. There were no visible signs of a major trauma. Touching his face, arms and chest I realized he was not sleeping. I couldn't make him get up and in fact, he was gone. As I talked to him, a tear formed on the inside of his left eye and I wiped it off with my finger. Soon a second tear formed in the exact same spot — the inside of his left eye. I wiped it away and said to him, *"It's okay Ronnie, don't cry... it will be okay."* I know this may sound rather strange to explain to you that I was talking to him but I thought then and know now that he could hear me. Not in the limited physical sense that we know of hearing but in a much deeper sense. My soul felt like he heard me. No other tears formed in his eyes during the thirty or so minutes I was alone with him.

I finally came to the realization that he was really gone and that secondly, he was okay. The time I spent alone with him was the most important gift I could have received. I needed to be alone with my son one more time before facing his babies and wife. My mind and heart were able to meet and the reality of his death began to sink in. I cannot find to this day, the words to explain my feelings regarding the depth of the loss of my son. We had so many years together and so many exceptional memories. The bond between us was so strong in life that I simply needed to think about him calling me and within an hour or two he was on the line. We were so attuned to each other that we didn't always need words to communicate but instead a look of understanding would pass between us and it spoke volumes.

I now understand the meaning of "gut wrenching." It was an actual physical pain in the gut area. It was like a punch to the stomach area that continues to hurt — badly for months. That was another word I had read many times in books and thought I knew the definition. I knew it in my head but not in my heart. Within the past eighteen hours I had internalized the words "surreal," "heart breaking" and "gut wrenching." It was just the beginning of my journey to understand loss and the chasm that existed between my head and my heart. The lyrics from Eric Clapton's song, "Tears in Heaven," "behind the door there's peace I'm sure…" just about said it all for me as the tears just kept running down my cheeks. Life would never be the same.

After leaving the funeral home we drove to Ronnie and Gina's home and watched as the young twins, and their older brother came running out to the car to greet us. The twins were so young and simply didn't understand. They knew Daddy wasn't home but time was not measurable to them. For all they knew, he might walk through the door in the next five minutes and grab them and hug them to his chest while laughing at their latest escapade! The irony of seeing the large butcher block paper sign they had all worked on the day before, with colored markers that said, "Welcome home Dad!" with the twins little squiggly lines on it was too much to bear. I still have the picture of that sign today in Ronnie's photo album. The look in Gina's eyes was devastating. Gina's mom had died from a traffic accident just over two years before. I was the only Mom left. I was the mother-in-law who tried to fix things and yet I was utterly powerless to fix this one. I now understand in my head and heart the meaning of another phrase, "being immobilized by grief."

I heard so many remarkable stories about Ronnie that were shared with me that started soon after our arrival late Monday afternoon and through the funeral on Saturday. People were coming over to the house to tell me about something special that he had done for them. One couple told me how he saved their marriage. Two older women said that when it snowed heavily in the mountains they never worried about getting to town to pick up groceries or their medicine because about 4:30 or 5:00 A.M. they would hear Ronnie's snow plow digging them out. He knew they relied on him and it sounded like he put them first on the list. I heard so many stories about specific things he had done to give people a helping hand. People continued to use the phrase that he seemed "bigger than life." One man said that he just couldn't believe Ronnie was gone. He said that if someone had told him World War III had broken out or that Ronnie was gone he would have more likely believed that a war had started.

One of the most startling discussions was with an older man who stopped by to talk to me around 7:00 P.M. Monday evening, soon after we arrived at the house. Although I had never met him before he was insistent that he meet with me. I remember thinking that I really didn't feel like talking with anyone I didn't know. Not yet at least, we had just left the funeral home. It was just too much. I was so emotionally spent and physically exhausted I just wanted to sit and escape into the silence of my mind. Not to be put off, he came into the house and sat at the dining room table patiently waiting to talk with me. Looking at this man with his weathered face, jeans and plaid shirt I wondered why he was being so insistent. He started to explain and over the next few minutes my perspective on Ronnie's death began a 180 degree turn! This man said he had been the last one to see Ronnie alive. He had driven up to the home site late Sunday afternoon, less than 24 hours earlier. Before continuing he looked away sadly and tried to compose himself. He told me that he and Ronnie were just talking and teasing each other and he mentioned to Ronnie to be careful on this particular piece of equipment. He pointed out to him that it was an old machine and didn't have a built in guard on it like the newer models. He went on to tell Ronnie that it had also been modified by the current owners and reiterated, yet again, the need to be careful. He said that as he drove home that evening he couldn't put his finger on it but that Ronnie just seemed so different. He said he seemed totally at peace and was listening intently to him as he cautioned him about the front loader. He said that Ronnie was not at all like his typical self, going a mile-a-minute. As he drove away from they property he said he had such a strange feeling and just couldn't identify it. He went on to say that when he heard about the accident later that evening, he understood why Ronnie sounded so different. He felt compelled to meet with me and explain. This total stranger wanted me to know about his last conversation with my son and even more importantly his distinct impression that Ronnie was so very different. He said he knew he needed to get to me as soon as I arrived in Dolores. A light switched on in my mind. After regaining my composure, I thanked him and told him I understood completely what he was describing because I had felt that exact way when I had talked to Ronnie earlier Sunday morning. I could hear the difference in his speech pattern, choice of words, basically everything. He sounded so gentle, not at all the rough and tumble type of guy that he usually projected. It had made such a significant impression on me that I had wished, at the time, that someone else would have been able to perceive the difference as well. Then I would be sure I wasn't letting my mind play tricks on me. Now, here was a man telling me he heard and even saw the significant change in my son. Was this a confirmation from God or the Universe that this was supposed to happen — that it wasn't simply an accident after all? What had caused both of us to notice it? What caused this tough mountain man whom I had never met until this evening, not be able to rest until he met me and shared his impressions with me. I needed more answers. Was this a message I was supposed to receive that Ronnie's death was part of his life script and not merely an accident? The possibility that it was 'meant to be' rattled around in my brain for months. Somehow I felt that if it was suppose to happen and not simply an accident that could have been prevented, it would be easier to accept. How could I know for sure? Sometimes the pragmatist in me thought, what does it matter, he is gone either way? But something in my very being refused to let me accept his death without delving deeper to figure out why. Now, eleven years later, I understand.

I flashed back to our conversation in his truck just a few weeks before when he asked me to be there for the boys if he should die. Did he have a premonition of impending death? Two months before the accident Ronnie and a friend had gone fishing on the Dolores River at daybreak one Saturday morning. He called me later, totally excited, not only about his trout catch but wanted to tell me about the incredible thing that had happened to him. He explained that as he was standing on the bank of the river and changing his bait, a Great Horned Owl not yet ready to end his nocturnal pursuits landed on a tree limb just above his head. It was so close that he could clearly see the markings on the stately bird. Better yet, he explained, it had dropped a feather that he had taken home. As he excitedly told me about the owl, I remember a shiver ran though me and I was unable to respond. My immediate thought was, please God don't let him tell me that he picked up the feather. But he did. In the 1970's and 1980's while I was in Denver and learning more about spiritualism, I had read some books about the various beliefs of Native American tribes involving animal symbols in nature. I remembered the significance of the owl and the feather. Impending death. Of everything I had studied years before, why did this exact piece of symbolism, of foreboding stay in my memory? I guess I knew on some level that I would need it later in my life. I was given the feather when I arrived at their home.

Destiny, by definition, means the seemingly inevitable succession of events in one's life that unfold. I had come to believe that I had written my own life script to learn specific lessons this go round. I also realized I had free will to take different turns in the road as they were presented. But when I look back now at the significant crossroads in my life I remember feeling compelled to move in a certain direction and at a specific speed. Maybe the Universe just has a way of presenting the easiest road for us to follow to learn the lessons we have decided upon and we can choose to take it or decide on an alternate route. I am beginning to believe, however, the alternate route is more difficult, more time consuming just like a detour that we sometimes have to take off a highway under construction.

Can you reflect back on the critical junctures in your life and relate to what I am saying? Didn't you just feel compelled to follow a certain path? I believe that is what is meant by living out our destiny. Regardless of the pathway we choose to take we usually arrive at our planned destination ultimately. We can't really abdicate the responsibility for the decisions we make along our life's journey. They are not the fault of others. But are, in fact, our decisions to make. Consequently, we are totally answerable for the results. The phrase, "the buck stops here," takes on a whole new meaning when you think of it in this context. I don't believe there are true victims in life because we have chosen our paths for the lessons and the knowledge we gain especially from the challenges and tragedies. Why is it that life can only be understood backwards but must be lived forward?

Ronnie's funeral was planned for Saturday, May 22, 1999. The fire department had an elk burger grill-out Thursday night since he had been a volunteer fireman. The love the community offered to all of us was truly overwhelming. I remember seeing pick-up trucks that had written in the back window, "In Memory of Ron." A billboard on the outside of town read the same. When you haven't really lived in a small town and you experience this kind of emotional support it can take your breath away. These were such wonderful people.

Since I was going to write and deliver the eulogy at the funeral, a minister had come over to meet with me. Another story was shared. It seemed that he and his wife had been on snowmobiles up in the mountains and had gotten stuck. He had walked to the road and hitched a ride down to Dolores and stopped at Ronnie's convenience store. The minister said he walked up to Ronnie (whom he had never met) and told him about his problem. He said Ronnie — going a mile a minute — just threw him the keys to his truck and said, *"Take my vehicle and go get your wife. We'll get the snowmobiles out when I get some time."* The minister said he was astounded! He said to me with an incredulous look in his eyes, *"He didn't even know me and he was giving me his keys!"* Later after getting the situation under control, and the rented snowmobiles returned, the minister came back to the store and ended up buying two snowmobiles for he and his wife. The minister told me that he had not even thought of buying them until Ronnie sold him on the idea. As I said earlier, he could sell bikinis to Eskimos, or in this case, snowmobiles to ministers!

At the funeral, over 110 flower arrangements were delivered to the funeral home. We had to place them on the front and back steps of the funeral home to have enough room inside. One man came up to me at the funeral and said he had only met Ronnie once but felt that he needed to be at the funeral because he respected him so much.

As a mother, all you can hope for is that you raise children that will make the world a little better place by being in it. My son did make the world a better place, without fanfare, without ever telling me what he was doing for whom, or how much he was contributing to help someone out. He simply did the right thing because it was the right thing. I am not only grateful but humbled by who he was before he passed on and who he is now. I am blessed to be his mom.

Gina and Ronnie had come up with the idea to build a playground/ park for the children in the community in memory of Gina's mother when she was killed in a traffic accident two years earlier. Unfortunately the funds at that time were not available. However, after Ronnie's death Gina pursued the dream again, and this time it became a reality. For people who wanted to do something in his memory the park needed to be built. Two years after Ronnie's death it was built for the children of the town. Gina had raised over $185,000 from individual donations and a Colorado state grant to finally build this amazing structure with slides, swings, climbing bars, bridges, and so much more. It sits right in front of the Dolores River and park. The community came out everyday for a week and physically built it under the guidance of Leather's and Associates, a design firm that believes in the community build concept. Community members who couldn't shovel rock or pound nails offered their support by supplying food — three meals a day — to all of us who were working. Today in Dolores, Colorado, you can see the F. Ronald Kotarski Jr. Memorial Community Playground in Joe Rowell Park. In addition to the enjoyment the children of this town have using it, students from surrounding school districts often take field trips to the park. It is absolutely beautiful and an incredible tribute to an incredible guy!

Ronnie always told me that he felt Dolores was "God's country." As I said in his eulogy, *"Ronnie was right, this is God's country not only because of the incredible surroundings but more importantly because of the people."*

Little did I know how God — the Universe — would direct me on my path over the next decade to experience my son with his "bigger than life personality" in a totally different way. Through the next ten plus years of my life, my head and heart once again have been connected to understand on a much deeper level the first law of thermodynamics that I referred to earlier: energy cannot be created nor destroyed — only changed in form.

What Is this Thing Called Grief?

I know we are more than this mere physical body that we have chosen to occupy. We are not a body with a spirit or soul but a spiritual being that has chosen a specific human body for the lessons we have chosen to learn. When the body itself is destined to fall away and the spirit is free, the energy of the spirit — the soul — continues to exist. The unconditional love that we have for each other doesn't leave us when the body is no longer, but continues because love transcends all. It is the alpha and omega, the beginning and the end — as we know it.

When we lose someone who is close to us we grieve. The stages of grief that Dr. Elizabeth Kübler-Ross developed: denial and isolation, anger, bargaining, depression and finally acceptance are not simply stages but can be emotional straitjackets that stop us from being fully present and living a full, blissful life. All of us experience these stages when we lose someone and the only variable is the length of time that we spend in each stage. We go through them at our own pace, as unique unto ourselves as our fingerprints. We may return to different stages during our grieving process because our hearts are so overwhelmed with our loss. We seem to experience an uncertainty about the future. After all, what can we really be sure of? Who will be here tomorrow? Will this "free floating" fear or feeling of devastation ever leave?

I have met people who are so locked into the stages of grief that sometimes years and years later their lives are, in essence, still on hold. Many times if you talk with them they will respond that they are still angry at the person who has passed on. Is this realistic? Do you believe the person that passed on would want you to be angry, depressed or simply to stop truly living? Suicides not withstanding, do you think your loved one wanted truly wanted to leave this earth? Remember, with the life scripts that we write we have chosen all of these experiences. You and your loved one agreed on these life experiences, including their death. They did not abandon you. Their lessons were learned. The unconditional love that you have for the individual is a gift that some people rarely experience. Be grateful for what was and confident of what is yet to be. You have more lessons to learn in life. We all do or we wouldn't be here. Invite the learning in and know that your loved one is with you always. I know letting go of the depression is hard work. But allowing yourself to be locked into any stage in the grief cycle is even harder work. Allowing yourself to remain stuck is unproductive and most of all both mentally and physically unhealthy.

I have been able to communicate with my son as well as my mother and sister since they have passed on. I have been aided by two people who are able to hear a different level of vibration than I could originally. When you are absorbed, immersed by the grief, it seems impossible to "hear" the messages from our loved ones regardless of how hard THEY try. Ronnie has told me that our loved ones, just behind the door, spend ninety percent of their energy trying to get our attention so they can communicate with us. It is time that we brought our fifty percent to the table.

I read an article in a popular magazine in which a woman was describing the death of her mother and subsequent reactions. As she sat by her mother's bedside she watched her take her last breath and immediately felt that her mother had been transformed into something different, more beautiful and seemed at peace. She said that she was not sure what this change was and could not label it but knew in her heart a transformation had taken place. Since her mother's death she explained that she has been drawn to walk outdoors and focus on the elements of nature when she feels the need to communicate with her. She added that she felt both happy and awed by what she had experienced. The emotion that she brought to her writing made it evident that she had experienced a surprising and wonderful gift. She was quick to point out that the idea of life after death was not only new to her but totally foreign to the belief system in which she was raised. She began to develop a worldview of inclusion — of more, not less — in her beliefs and created her own hybrid.

She found peace and a connection in nature. When is the last time you have gone for a walk to just relax and appreciate all that nature has to offer? Have you noticed the fluttering of a butterfly or moth? Sometimes we feel compelled to just stop and observe it to see if it will land. Butterflies often bring a smile to our face. They just seem joyous about their existence. Butterflies and moths are excellent analogies to our own lives. They help us visualize similarities, differences and transformations. The four distinct stages of these insects: egg, larva/caterpillar, pupa/chrysalis and adult demonstrate the amazing metamorphoses or transitions that take place during lifetimes. We also have four stages of development: birth, childhood, adolescence/young adult and adult. Just as children, the larva or caterpillar physically grows at an incredible speed but are limited in their deeper understanding due to a more contained environment and fewer life experiences. Even their shapes and movements reflect those of a young child, slower, plodding and a bit unsteady. But the lessons they learn and the job they do is so important at this stage that it is literally life or death for the next stage. When we see a pupa or chrysalis, it appears as if nothing is happening,; it appears immobile but immense changes are taking place on the inside. Sometimes when we observe young adolescents it may appear as if not much is happening or, at least, that not much is making an impression in their minds. They are taking everything in, however, weighing their observations with preconceived notions and trying to make sense out of life. They are working internally, preparing and nurturing themselves for the huge transition into adulthood. As adults, our physical bodies stop using the immense energy to grow and we are compelled to redirect the energy to develop our skills and our mental and emotional strength. Just as human beings, there are so many varieties in moths and butterflies but all have predictable ages and stages in their lives. The dull colored moth has a fuzzy body and prefers to come out at dark, but seems driven in a frenzied, erratic pattern toward the light. When resting they keep their wings flat against their bodies to protect themselves and to keep the world out. By comparison, butterflies come in a rainbow of colors and sizes. Each one seems to be more beautiful than the one before. Their body is graceful with intriguing patterns on their wings. They are not only active during the daylight hours but seem to bring a light feeling — a smile — to those who see them. They even act inquisitive as they fly around and occasionally land as if to greet us. The butterfly hold its' wings vertically, or open, and seems to be inviting in possibilities. As humans we can learn a great deal from the many amazing creatures of nature. Wouldn't it wonderful if we could emulate the butterfly with its purposeful energy, inquisitive nature and their light, happy existence and make the world smile just from our existence.

Seeking a sanctuary in nature, meditation or any unique way that draws more positive energy to you is an important element in healing your heart. Remember the saying, seek and ye shall find. It absolutely applies here. After we get through the initial shock and early stages of grieving for our loved one, we may want to find a way to communicate with them. Just as the woman learned to communicate with her mother by walking in nature, we must find our own unique way. Find something that brings you tranquility or even just a mental escape so that you can bit-by-bit eliminate the negative reflections about your loss that slips back into your mind. When we change our routine and do something different that is rejuvenating, it is not time wasted but time invested in our mental and physical health. It enables us to open the doors of our mind to possibilities. Life just seems a little brighter. Each of us needs to find our own special way to connect to something outside of our regular routines. It puts life in perspective and helps us realize the many positives we still have left in our lives. Time spent in our own sanctuary helps lighten the load of the emotional baggage that we have been carrying. Finding this refuge, this peace, is essential. It will help you let go of the fear-based depression and anger that locks your loved one out and locks you in, immersed in your sorrow. Think of it as a positive distraction in your life that will give your wounded heart a little time to heal. There are no blue ribbons, or best in show awards for keeping yourself in limbo. My question to you is — are you allowing yourself to get stuck in the anger or denial stage that Dr. Kübler-Ross talks about so clearly? If so, what good is it doing you and your loved ones both near and far. What is truly your greatest fear about letting go of the negative emotions you are feeling? Holding on to the negative memories involved in losing your loved one for fear that without these memories you would have nothing left is counterproductive. Your fear, anger or depression is analogous to a moth that has been captured in a glass jar. It flies around erratically hitting the sides of the jar in a fruitless effort to get out. The walls of the jar are like the emotional walls that you may have erected to protect yourself. Like the moth, you may be expending all of your emotional energy in a self-perpetuating cycle. Get rid of the restrictions and limitations that you have surrounded yourself with by mentally opening the lid of the jar and allowing trust once again to enter your world. You will then be able to expand your view of loss to include the light of knowing that communication with your loved one is not only possible but probable when you are emotionally ready. Change your perspective and change your life. Visualize a garden of butterflies each inviting you to observe their brilliance as they fly around you and encircle you with light, love and truth.

Please don't emulate the behavior of the rabbit in <u>Alice in Wonderland.</u> Remember when they are talking about having opinions and Alice says, 'You can't have an opinion on that... you don't have any information' The rabbit replies, 'Of course I can... that is what an opinion usually is!' Have you ever noticed that when someone gives you an opinion on something that you disagree with and you ask them for actual facts to back it up they simply respond, "I just know it" or "That's just the way it is." Really? Frequently, their lack of information is simply an unwillingness to expend the mental energy necessary to learn about something in greater depth. I feel strongly that opinions, based on little or no information, is simply the opiate of the masses. Don't let yourself fall into this category. Loss, in itself, is difficult enough to deal with. Refuse to let your mind be held captive by what was and do the work to discover what is and what can be. Keep your mind open to possibilities in life. Do more, seek more, be more — not less. Get up and get going. Find out what is waiting for you when you seek a greater truth. You will be amazed at what unfolds.

You can find a way, your own unique way, to reconnect just as I have done. Meditation and prayer cannot be overstated as ways to help us focus our thinking and eliminate the static or negatives in our mind. They allow us to connect to a higher level of energy or vibration. I have experienced this for over a decade. Our loved ones are with us, around us, and trying to guide us all the time. To achieve this level of belief takes work but is so worth it! To mentally surround yourself with positives and to train yourself to think positively about life is a challenge. Life is tough! We are immersed in a sea of emotions. It is so easy — too easy actually — to fall into the habit of negative thinking. Just remember life involves two basic emotions, love and fear. I try to remember that love draws things to me and fear pushes things away. It is that simple and complex simultaneously.

Due to years and years of programming, replaying the mental tapes in our heads of "believe this, not that," "do this, not that" has made us skeptical, maybe even closed to something that is unseen. Well, air is unseen right? But we know it is around us. Some people have a fear of anything remotely connected with 'the other side.' I understand how this happens. If you have watched any TV programs or movies lately on the topic you will notice that eerie sounding music is often interspersed as the plot is being acted out. That could unnerve anyone. It is truly a shame that fear sells so well in our society.

For your own sake and to be able to reconnect and honor the unconditional love from your loved ones on the other side, I pray that you will be inspired to trust, have faith in the unseen and to believe in the occasional "nudge" we hear, feel or see that reminds us they are near.

Believe me, for the longest time I thought that when I get to the other side, I wanted to talk with God and ask him — Why??? Why did a perfectly healthy, thirty-six-year old father have to be taken in the prime of his life leaving his young children, wife and family? Then I would have to stop and remind myself that God or the Universe doesn't make mistakes. Only we, as physical beings on this Earth, seem to be in that position due to the gift and burden of free will.

Now through my faith and experiences, I have an absolute certainty that Ronnie and my mom and sister not only live on, granted in a different form, but are here with me at all times. Yes, I would love to see Ronnie in his jeans, shirt and work boots again. But I know if I could see him even one more time, it would not be enough and I would become fixated on seeing him again and again. That would stop my life's work in its' tracks. When we let go of the why's, the anger and the depression, we are able to begin hearing and seeing that life just has a way of working out. Ronnie mentioned that when he thinks of us it is like looking at a photo album with wonderful pictures of us together and the unused or blank pages will be filled in later when we are once again together.

We are not in the position of being the Grand Designer. Believe me, I would have signed up at the beginning if that position were posted as an opening! Through a deeper understanding we are given the opportunity to respond with greater knowledge, faith and love as we experience this roller coaster called life. It is not for the faint of heart. But it is for a reason. We don't have to like it, we just have to do it. Remember when your parents told you to do some task in the house or yard that needed to be done (maybe weeding the flower garden) and you talked under your breath that you didn't want to stop what you were doing and complete the chore they pointed out. It still had to be done.

To me, it boils down to this: We can go through life saying, why me? Why did I have to lose the most precious thing I had in life? We can rail that life is so unfair. We can even be angry, allow yourself some time to acknowledge that you have a right to be angry. You have lost someone and you are truly alone with that grief in your heart. Just don't get stuck because of the void you feel. Sometimes, it seems to take most of our lifetime to realize that none of us will be able to avoid the pain, the hurt and the devastation of losing a loved one. The challenge is what we do after that measures us as a person.

Speaking of this, have you ever noticed that even in the huge bookstores there are only a few — maybe two- or three-small shelves — on the topic of death? Trust me on this one. I have actually counted the number of books on the topic in two major bookstore chains to be sure this wasn't just in my imagination. I realize many people may not pick up a book on the topic for nighttime leisure reading. But likewise to keep one's head buried in the sand, knowing we will all experience this sooner or later, seems a tad naïve to me. Maybe books on the topic aren't usually best sellers so there is no corporate interest in pursuing a larger collection. Pity though, don't you think? I would prefer to be prepared rather than blindsided.

By further reading, studying, and making the connections with our loved ones on the other side, we are able to reach an awareness that their spirit is still with us and we can play the cards we are dealt with greater understanding, love and faith in the Universe, in God. We are not, in fact, alone. We have not lost them. Let go and let your unconditional love bring them to you. Their energy is all around us.

When you meet people who are aloof and want to keep you at arm's length you can feel it, right? You can feel their energy sort of pushing you away. It almost makes you want to back up a step or two when talking with them. It feels like they have drawn a protective shield around them. Often, these people are insecure or afraid to let anyone get close to them. Maybe they have been hurt in the past and can't let go of it. Similarly, I believe that grief puts up an invisible wall of energy around us. We keep people away many times because it hurts less than to have them see us break down.

That same wall we put around ourselves serves not only to keep those on this side away from us but also those on the other side away. Through our unconditional love and belief that energy cannot be created nor destroyed only changed in form, we allow our loved ones on the other side to open the doors in our mind and be able to communicate with us. I know because I experience it everyday.

Premonition —
The Collective Unconscious

Six weeks before Ronnie's death, we were in Colorado visiting them. We had already made all the arrangements to take a family vacation to Disney World for the first week of June. We were all so excited and talking nonstop about it. I could sense that Ronnie was preoccupied. Something was on his mind and he seemed a bit on edge. After watching him for a couple days I asked him to take me to their new home site. It was unusual for me to suggest going alone with him and not taking the rest of the family. Something just told me that we needed to be alone for an hour or so. He seemed happy to be with me but continued to be a combination of touchy and preoccupied. As we drove up the long dirt driveway to the building site I could see how proud he was that their dreams were actually taking shape. He wanted so badly to build this house for his family. He had previously purchased eleven acres and the house was now in the initial framing stage. The elevation of the house would allow close to a 360 degree view of the La Plata mountains on the east, Mesa Verde on the south, The Sleeping Ute mountains on the west and the Blue mountains toward the northwest. The view was absolutely breathtaking! I don't know of any place I have traveled to that has the beauty and majesty of the Rocky Mountains. He walked me through the bottom floor since it was a walk out design and showed me where each of the three boys would have their own rooms and then showed me the extra bedroom on this level. In the middle of this area was a large playroom with a huge tree trunk, about ten-feet tall and thirty-inches in diameter that was used as one of the support beams. It was just as I would have expected his home to be like — part mountain — part nature — with room for his boys to play. I remember having to climb on beams to see the next level and Ronnie was so worried about me falling. He was careful to hold my hand and guide me so I wouldn't slip. It was coming together beautifully. He was full of possibilities as he discussed their plans for the property.

He and Gina had designed the house on paper so it was definitely a family vision and as it looked at that point, soon to become a reality. Ronnie had been in the small town of Dolores for over ten years and had rebuilt the convenience/liquor store from the ground up. He knew building construction and had become friends with so many people that being able to oversee the project and knowing who to hire to do the specialty items would be easy for him. We spent thirty minutes or so just walking around on the bottom level, climbing up the make-shift stairs to the platform on the second level and talking. I told him that I was so proud of what he had accomplished in his life and how excited I was to see the house actually taking shape. He was beaming. We are all motivated when we hear and feel positive energy and enthusiasm from someone we love, especially our parents.

When we got back into "old brown" to drive the ten minutes or so back to their existing home, I didn't want to dampen his spirit but I felt I needed to talk to him about his recent demeanor. I told him I was concerned about him and that he seemed a combination of agitated and preoccupied, just out of character. I asked him if there was anything I could do. He said, *"No Mom, everything is okay."* As we pulled up into the driveway I told him that maybe seeing a counselor might help. This was the first and only time I had ever mentioned something like that to him.

His usual macho demeanor would have been to immediately discount such a suggestion and say something like, "A shrink?? Are you kidding Mom! Do you think I'm crazy? I don't need to talk to anyone, I'm fine." But he didn't respond that way at all. He just looked directly into my eyes and said calmly. *"Do you really think I need to talk to someone?"*

I told him, yes, I thought it might help and that I was just worried that he didn't seem totally himself. Maybe because he had so much on his plate with all the businesses, the new house being built, his family — maybe because of a lot of things — it just might help. I felt like a cloud was hanging over his head. I had never seen him like this before. The difference was noticeable to me.

We had returned to the house and as he turned the key to shut off the truck he again looked me straight in the eye and took my breath away with his next comment. *"Mom, just promise me something."* I said, *"Of course, Hon, what is it?"* He said, *"Promise me that if I die, you will take care of my boys."* He said Gina would be okay but that she would need help with the three kids. I was flabbergasted! I said, *"Ronnie, don't talk that way, nothing is going to happen to you, you aren't going to die. I will go first, I'm older, I'm the Mom, I am suppose to die first."* He looked at me with an immediate flash of anger in his hazel eyes and said, *"Mom, don't ever say that again. I couldn't live without you in my life!"*

This emotion, this conversation coming from a son who emulated John Wayne was so incongruous to his personality that I was absolutely shocked and rendered speechless. He went on to say that I was to be sure that the boys received his fifty-percent interest in all the stores and mentioned other business interests so that that they would have everything they needed. I told him that he would never have to ask me to take care of the boys that I would do everything I possibly could do to be a part of their lives because they were my grandchildren. There was simply no need to ever ask.

As quickly as the conversation started it ended. He simply said, *"Thanks Mom, I love you"* and opened the door of "old brown" to get out. It was remarkable to hear these statements coming from him and even more remarkable that his mood immediately changed after our conversation. He was himself again. The dark cloud that seemed to have dampened his spirits disappeared. The image flashed in my mind of a man carrying a huge sack over his shoulders, weighing him down as his body sagged slightly from the weight and then watching the same man toss aside the heavily laden sack and stand more erect walking forward with renewed energy. As I was getting out of the truck I had to force my body to move. I was dumb-founded by not only what he said but the way he said it. I thought about this strange conversation. This was not the child I raised. I ran the conversation over and over in my mind. I thought about his circumstances. He was thirty-six-years old, a father with tremendous responsibilities to his family who also had a plethora of business demands. Maybe he was concerned about the eventuality of when we all leave this earth or…. I wasn't sure what the blank was. I just knew I had heard something come out of him that I could never, ever have imagined.

The artist, Bill Withers wrote a song entitled, "Lean On Me" and the words spoke to me as I was thinking about what Ronnie had just said, "We all need somebody to lean on." We had always been there for each other and I was not sure what lay ahead.

Over the past decade I have learned more about communication of this type and I am convinced that he was communicating all of this unwittingly to prepare me, to help me get through his death six weeks later. I think he was letting me know that there was a plan in this Universe and I needed to be able to accept it when it happened. I know this sounds strange to say but I don't think he was aware of his impending death but on a more subconscious level was directed to prepare me. Our love was so strong for each other. We had each other's backs as the phrase goes. Many times in our lives it was just us — together — and we dealt with life as it came crashing into us. However, we kept each other safe and knew together we could accomplish just about anything. We used to laugh and say we were each others' greatest critics and greatest supporters.

As I was reading about messages that seemed to come to people out of the blue, I ran across an explanation that reverberated in me. N. Carl Jung referred to the collective unconscious as a pool of knowledge that is available to people in the depths of their psyche. He said it is an inherent part of our brain structure. He further explained that it is the shared unconscious of all humanity. This was hard for me to conceptualize but I couldn't let it go. Was this information that Ronnie was so intent upon sharing coming from the collective unconscious? Is that where a premonition originates?

So many times in the first two years after his passing, I had closed my eyes and gone back to that conversation. It seems I had replayed the tape a million times in my mind. The "what ifs" and "if onlys" would pop in from time to time but then my mind and heart would begin to function together and I would get back to reality. There are no mistakes in this world. I don't have to like it, agree with it or even understand it, but as Ronnie has told me so many times since his death, *"all is as it should be."* Knowing this doesn't replace a son but it does help to stop the profuse bleeding of your heart.

When someone says they feel like their heart is breaking, I understand. I stop, look and LISTEN to them with empathy and compassion. By definition, heart breaking means overwhelming sorrow — and it is. I see it in the eyes of so many of my friends who have lost a loved one. Once you live through 'overwhelming sorrow' it's as if you have a heightened sensitivity to it in others. You can see that the depth of their hurt reflects the depth of their humanity and love for the individual who has passed on.

The conversation, guidance and love that I experience from Ronnie, my mom and sister might sound like it is too impossible to believe. I understand that. Again, I just ask that if you are in that mindset, please continue reading and suspend judgment until you are finished with this book. You may or may not change your thinking. The gift of choice is always up to you.

The title of this book is actually a phrase that Ronnie has used often over the last decade, *We are just behind the door.* For me, the symbolism of the door is important for many reasons. The door to our homes can be opened or closed. Inviting contact and communication in, from the world, or closed, shutting ourselves off to possibilities. We can also think of this symbolism as doors in our minds, which can be open in a present tense or closed in the past tense. If we genuinely trust ourselves enough to open the door to a belief in what others might think impossible, the results can be healing and affirming. Our loved ones' life on this earth had a purpose. Their transformation to the other side also had a purpose. Part of their purpose is to show us that our unconditional love allows communication with them to continue.

Seeking Answers —
Receiving Messages

In 1971, I began studying, as an avocation, the purpose of life, what happens when we die and why; I thought, life was so unfair to some — particularly my sister. My earliest recollection of these questions goes back even further, however, to the mid 1960s. My maternal grandmother had her own gift in seeing behind the door. Although she would never have wanted to be referred to as a reader, and refused to read for money because she was a Catholic, she had the gift. She would frequently tell different family members things that she thought they needed to know.

As a young child around five or six, I remember staying overnight a few times with Grandma and once in bed would begin to hear unusual sounds and feel breezes that would even move the bedroom curtains. I would ask her what was happening and she would just answer quietly that it was just her spiritual family and friends who had come to say hello. I was never afraid because she was so matter-of-fact about it. I just wanted to actually see them. She told me I would understand more about it as I got older. My sisters who were eleven-years older than I were scared to death and didn't want to talk with me about it. When I would ask my mom she would also dismiss it and simply say, 'that's just Grandma, don't worry about it." I wasn't exactly worried but I did want some explanation. None was forthcoming.

When Ronnie was about four-years old he and I would make our weekly Saturday visits to the German bakery to get grandma pumpernickel bread. She loved it with everything, especially Limburger cheese. She would offer us a piece and the smell of the cheese alone would cause you to step back a pace or two while searching for a polite way to decline.

She was a short, blond, blue-eyed German by birth who was adopted and never knew her biological parents. At her zenith she was around 4'11" and wore her long, blond hair in a bun, pulled back tightly from her face. She was a seamstress and worked in clothing factories as well as sewed piece work at home. She would sew amazing dresses for women and was truly appreciated for her skill. She married a Frenchman who worked in the coal mines in Ohio. They had four children and settled into a small town in Michigan. My grandfather died in his early 40's from black lung disease. I never met, in fact, either grandfather. Both died at young ages from the same disease. I don't know how old Grandma was when she was able to see things into the future. Maybe she always could. She would lay a deck of regular playing cards down and voila! She would tell me to go into the other room. Being an inquisitive young child I would strain to hear through the walls of the dining room what she was saying to the family member sitting at her kitchen table. I wasn't interested in the information she was sharing but was absolutely fascinated that she could do it. I know that when she was alone she would use these same cards and read — or hear — information about others. One thing for certain, when Grandma told you something — listen carefully! She never read the cards for me but would just mention something in passing about my life that would surprise me. I would always ask her how she knew it and she would reply, "*A little bird told me*" and leave it at that.

I was twenty-six-years old and remarried one month when I went to

Grandma's house on Saturday to deliver the fresh bread. She said to me, *"You are moving far, far away from me and you will have a big dog."* Shocked, I simply responded, *"Oh, Grandma, I'm not going anywhere. I have my teaching job here and a house and haven't even thought of moving."* Grandma just gave me a serious look and with her misty blue eyes repeated, *"You are leaving me, you are moving far away."* I remember thinking how ridiculous that sounded as I drove home that afternoon. Within a couple of days my husband announced that he had sent in an application to a college in the Denver area and they wanted to interview him! I had absolutely no idea he had applied for a job out of state. He added that if it all worked out we would have to move within a month. Due to my mom's urging, I had bought my parents' house from them six months earlier when I was still single. They were going to follow the sun to Arizona in their retirement.

My parents were the only ones to have moved out of a radius of twenty-five miles from our birthplace. They had retired and moved to Prescott, Arizona, to relieve the pain of Mom's osteoarthritis. The idea of leaving my family and friends and moving to Colorado was not something that had even entered by mind. I was not remotely interested but didn't feel I had a choice. Being newly married I thought that if that was what my husband wanted I needed to go along with it. Within two weeks he was officially hired. This meant I needed to find renters for the house I had bought from Mom and Dad, and find a job and house in Denver— and fast! Since it was summer and staffing for districts is most often completed as early in June as possible I knew speed was of the essence. I was directing a summer school program at the time and could only take two days off. Driving nineteen hours nonstop over an extended weekend, I interviewed at a school district in a northern suburb of Denver AND put a down payment on a house. It sounds terribly rash to buy a house as my mother would say, on a wing and a prayer, but I knew we needed a place to live and I simply had to get a job to help with expenses. I had not been officially hired, but just knew it would happen. I looked at about six houses on Saturday and found one that would work and was in our price range. But, there was one hitch. It seemed that the older couple that owned the house was also moving to Arizona and would only sell it if I agreed to take their Alaskan Malamute with the house. They explained that it would be much too hot to take a dog like that to Arizona. The house was a good buy and in a nice location … . I agreed to take the dog.

Three weeks later, I was driving the car and following the rental truck, which held all our worldly possessions, and we were on our way to Colorado. I remember tears running down my cheeks all the way across the never-ending flatlands of Iowa and Nebraska. Highway 80 seemed like it went on forever since the governor on the truck maximized our speed at fifty-two-miles per hour. The word 'guano' kept coming to me and it seemed a fitting description for the endless drive across those states and this ultimate move. I didn't want to leave my family, especially my sister, or the security I felt in the familiar Michigan setting. Somewhere between Omaha and Lincoln, Nebraska I remembered Grandma's message to me. I was beyond shaken and determined to figure out what this gift was that enabled her to see things in the future.

See You Later —
My Sister, My Friend

After settling in Denver it helped when a few months later we met a group of people who were looking for another couple to add to their monthly canasta group. It seemed there were more people who had moved to Denver than natives, so friendship was, oftentimes, as close as family. I loved my teaching assignment in the new school system. The house was working out quite well and the dog seemed just fine with his new family. There were good things about the move but the one thing that kept tugging at my heart strings was not being able to see my sister, Phyllis. She and I talked occasionally by phone, which helped fill the 1,200 miles of loneliness that separated us. The feelings of isolation between us could vanish with the ringing of the phone. For the entire twenty years I lived in Denver, her life seemed to be one of continuous challenge. She seemed to have so many things happen to her that appeared to be just downright unfair.

She always took immaculate care of herself. Her brown hair was fashioned in an upsweep and her makeup highlighted her beautiful, but sad, big brown eyes. She worked in a paper mill, eight hours a day standing on concrete floors, in the nasty heat and humidity of Michigan summers and the icy cold winters. There was no such thing as temperature control in the plant. It was unheard of in that era. When visiting in the summer in the early 1970s, I had stopped by a couple of times during her fifteen-minute break period and experienced the environment myself. You would have had to see it to believe it. I still don't know how she tolerated it. The loud, repetitious pounding of the machines and the speed of which the workers were expected to work as the paper cartons flew by them on the conveyor belt was too much for me. If the factory setting didn't kill you it seemed the extreme heat or cold would. However, she was not one to complain and just continued to work and help 'make ends meet.' I don't think she ever thought she had other options in life.

Eventually, she became a union stewardess who was so good at resolving employee issues that the company tried to hire her into management. Sadly, she allowed herself to be talked out of this opportunity by a family member who didn't want her to lose the 'protection of the union.' She would have been a tremendous asset to any team. She was a defender of the underdog but had the ability to redirect employees if they were pushing beyond what was truly fair to the company. In seemed she could stand up for others, but not for herself. When it came to her personal life she was fearful of so many, many things, especially of being alone. She endured a great deal to avoid the prospect of ever living alone. Sometimes, I think due to her poor relationship with our dad she never developed a sense of self worth. It was so sad. She was such a wonderful, giving human being who had a sharp mind and a repartee for one-liners that could hit the center core of a target, bounce back and hit it again.

Her health was beginning to deteriorate and her marriage, good in the beginning, was slowly unraveling. When you combine all of these issues with the responsibilities and constant worry involved in raising her children and step-children, life was just overwhelming. The relationship she had with her twin sister... well, there just aren't words to describe that dynamic! They were identical twins but had very different views on life. Often when she simply had to unload and had forgotten about the time change she would call about 2:00 A.M. I remember thinking all this time, why can't she just get a break in life? Why is life so incredibly difficult for her?

I combined my fascination with my grandma's gift with my concern about my sister's life and began to question many things I had been taught or had just taken for granted. Seeking answers, I enrolled in evening classes and workshops on topics dealing with the esoteric. During this period things began to happen to me that still surprise me. It was as if the Universe was opening to me and giving me answers to questions as yet unasked. One night Phyllis called crying and said, *"Guess what?"* I responded, *"You're pregnant."* She was shocked and said, *"How did you know?"* I told her I didn't and that I didn't know what made me say it. She confirmed that she was pregnant but was afraid that at forty-years old and with her health issues — she wouldn't be able to really take care of another child. I told her I would do my half and that everything would work out. We laughed and cried together and a beautiful baby girl was brought into this world seven months later.

Another time, she called me and said, *"Guess what?"* I said, *"You bought new carpeting."* She said, *"Okay smart ass, what color is it?"* I said, *"It's off-white upstairs and orange downstairs."* She said, *"I hate it when you do that."* I said that I was sorry and meant it. I didn't consciously think before these comments would come blurting out of my mouth. Due to my perception at the time, that her life was so difficult and unfair, I continued to search for answers in life. I took even more classes in the evenings and at one point did the mathematical calculations for a man who read horoscope charts. In return he was helping me understand what astrology was all about. Now, of course, there are software programs to crunch your birth time, date, location and spit out a pretty nifty looking chart about the uniqueness of you. During this period the questions kept nagging at me. How did Grandma 'see' into the future? Why is life so unfair to my sister? I felt if I could just find some answers maybe I could help my sister.

As I continued reading authors such as Edward Casey, Hugh Lynn Casey, Ruth Montgomery, Raymond Moody, Brian Weiss, Betty Eadie, and later Sylvia Browne, John Edward, Deepak Chopra, Elisabeth Kübler-Ross, Shirley MacLaine, James Van Praagh and Hollister Rand, to name a few, but important authors, I began to internalize what they were saying.

We have each chosen our particular life path for the lessons we need to learn. The greatest of which is unconditional love for self and others. Well, as I thought about this in my mind it began to make sense. It at least helped me understand why some people have so much more to contend with in life. Wow! Then I discovered that when the lessons were presented, if you do not learn them they would come back around and as Ronnie used to say, "and bite you in the butt!" If a lesson isn't learned the first time, each subsequent time it is presented it seems to be in a more dramatic or difficult way to get your attention so that you will understand and hopefully learn it. It is as if the Universe first whispers the lesson to be learned and if that doesn't resonate with us, the volume is turned up to a raised voice and finally a roar. The Universe just has a way of getting our attention sooner or later.

Almost on cue, as my understanding about the big questions in life grew, I began to see that my own situation was becoming even more challenging. What was this lesson I was supposed to be learning? It seemed that the more questions I asked, the greater the challenges became. At one point I actually entertained the thought that it would be easier to keep my head buried in the sand and not seek any more answers but I just didn't have it in my personality to do so. The box in my mind had been tightly sealed earlier in my life and it had finally been thrown open. I felt driven to continue questioning and learning. I remember thinking that I was fortunate not to have lived during the historical period of the Inquisition. As misdirected and unfortunate as this event was, I would have been found guilty of seeking answers to the unanswered questions in life and would not have lived to see tomorrow!

It was the late 1970s and the spousal thing just wasn't working for my son or for me. If you don't feel that your spouse loves your child unconditionally and accepts him for who he is, you can become defensive, overly protective and begin to withdraw. It's a package deal.

For many of those reasons and others, I knew a change had to be made. I had also come to realize that for some men it was too threatening to have a wife that made more money than they did. To me it didn't matter. To them, it gave them an excuse to do less, which in turn caused me to work harder, and as they say, the wheel went round and round until both exhaustion and resentment set in.

Looking back on my life, I realize that like my sister, I always wanted to make people happy regardless of the toll it took on me. Selflessness was revered in our background and early religious training. One of the actual lessons I had to learn was to take care of myself as well. I must have been one of those slow learners. It took me a long time to figure out that when airline personnel tell you to be aware of the exit paths, seat belts and to put your own oxygen mask on first before helping your child, there is a good reason. It is a great metaphor for life. You need to take care of self first so you will be strong enough when needed to help others.

This lesson seemed paired with another lesson that I am also still working on: to learn to say, "No," and not be worried if the other person's feelings are hurt or they are disappointed. Raised with an alcoholic father who was physically abusive to my mother and sister, I became conditioned to avoid conflict at all cost and just try to keep everyone happy. Unfortunately, I had perfected this approach to an art form! Now I know that this approach eventually robs people of the lessons they were put on this earth to learn and simultaneously feeds the ego in us. It is sobering, to say the least, when you realize that you are doing things for your own ego gratification. I truly was unaware of this for most of my adult life. Not a good realization to discover about yourself, but nonetheless an important one.

In 1972, my German grandmother died. I felt so badly that I couldn't afford to fly back to the funeral. I was quite naïve and not aware that the age of instant money (in the form of a loan) had become a common approach. My attitude about not borrowing money, except for a home or car loan, could have been attributed to my mother's early programming that "You don't spend what you don't have." Regardless, I didn't make the funeral and felt terrible about it. I just couldn't let it go from my mind. As I said earlier my grandma would say, "a little bird told me," when you would ask her how she "knew" something. For three or four days after her death, a little brown sparrow came and perched on the brick windowsill in my dining room in Denver. At first I thought he was hurt but as I watched him move about he appeared fine. He just wouldn't leave. Even if you walked up to the window and tapped on it he stubbornly stayed put. Now I was really getting upset. Was this Grandma's way of telling me I blew it? Finally, I went to the Catholic church a few blocks away to say a prayer for her. While I was on my knees, praying and feeling badly that I couldn't honor her by going back to Michigan for the funeral, I heard a voice say, *"Stop crying, it's just an old body in an old box!"* Even though it was midday there were other people in the church. I quickly looked around to see if anyone else heard it. It had been pretty loud to me. Nope, just me. It sounded just like the words and intonation that my grandma used! She was a no-nonsense type of person, who, like my mom, was a woman of few words — and meant every one of them. I guess you could say this was my first direct experience of 'hearing' from a loved one on the other side.

During spring break in 1973, Ronnie and I drove home to Michigan to see my sister and family. I asked her to take me to Grandma's grave. I wanted to pay my belated respect and remember the good times we had. Phyllis agreed and drove me to the cemetery, stopped near the gravesite, pointed and said, *"It's a little ways down there."* She said she would be back in half an hour and just drove off! I walked down the rows searching for her burial stone. I became discouraged as I walked around and couldn't locate it and then, there it was, only two feet away from me. I stood there and thought about so many things. She was a strong and unusual person. When I left Michigan and moved to Denver she was eighty-seven-years old. Everything about her four-foot, ten-inch frame and tight, blond bun let you know she was still in charge. She was an excellent cook, baker and seamstress. She was well known for the smell wafting from her house of baking bread. Three absolutely perfect loaves of white bread came out of her wood-burning oven every week. I often wondered while watching her, how does she know exactly how much kindling to put in the stove? She knew and somehow you just didn't dare question her. On Saturdays, when Mom worked in a retail clothing store, she would drop me off at her house. Grandma would let my cousin and me take the empty Pepsi bottles back to the store and get the refund, two cents per bottle. We were always excited as the pennies mounted up and we could afford to buy a box of macaroni and cheese for fifteen cents for lunch. When Grandma fixed it for us it always tasted absolutely delicious. Now, as I think about it I'm sure it was the extra butter she used. We felt pretty lucky on those Saturdays. We knew she loved us even though hugs or kisses were never a part of her behavior.

After the thirty-minute visit at her gravesite, I walked back up the small path to the driveway to meet my sister. She drove up and said, *"What did you think?"* Again, without even thinking, I opened my mouth and said to her, *"Why did you let them put a necklace around her neck for the burial? You know she always hated necklaces and thought that they felt like they were choking her!"* My poor sister, burst out crying and said, *"I told Barbara (her twin) not to do that but she wouldn't listen."* Again, I apologized profusely and said I didn't know what caused me say it. I hadn't even been thinking about anything like that when I was visiting her grave. It seemed that when it came to a few people I felt close to in life, without thinking, I would blurt things out — coming from where I didn't know — but accurate things none-the-less that would totally unnerve them.

My sister who I communicate with from the other side will always be my forever friend and confidant. She and I were so close for most of our lives that it is hard to adequately describe the bond we shared. I believe we have had many lives together. (Reincarnation is not quite as difficult to understand when you communicate with those just behind the door.) I told her once that the next time we decided to reincarnate we were going to use a ghostwriter (no pun intended) to write our script. We must have had a tendency to throw in everything but the kitchen sink and think, 'sure we can learn this and this and this' and the challenges in life just kept building up and getting harder and harder.

I remember my mom referring to my sisters, who were eleven years older than I, as a 'healthy twin and a sickly twin.' They were born in 1933 when the detection of childhood diabetes was still rare. Consequently, Mom was unaware at the time that my sister, Phyllis, had sugar issues from a young age and that was a huge part of her being the 'sickly one.'

She was on dialysis for four hours, three times per week before she passed on. For those of you who have not had any experience with dialysis let me just say I think it is inhumane. Most patients seem to get weaker each time they go in for a treatment. It physically hurts, especially for those who can't afford the numbing cream before they insert the needle. You have a set time to be there and a specific chair to be in. Frequently a patient goes in for their treatment and looks over at a chair of someone they have come to know and it is vacant. At first they ask, where is 'John' today? Later on they don't ask because the answer is the same. John is gone. Overall, I think it is worse than cancer. At least with cancer there is a possibility given the latest research that the medical profession can find a cure for your specific type and stage. If you are on dialysis, medically fragile and without a family match for a kidney, you just get progressively worse and are basically, "shit out of luck" as my dad would say. Your chances of getting better in my opinion are basically zero to none.

Phyllis had been in and out of the hospital so many times and lately had gotten to the point that she wasn't even eating very much. The doctors' ordered two separate CAT scan procedures to see if anything could be done. The technician doing the procedures at the hospital missed the notation in her file that indicated she was in renal failure. He used a less costly type of contrast dye during the scans. After the second test followed by a dialysis treatment administered at the hospital she became basically unresponsive for five days. In layman's terms, the dye remained in her brain since she did not have functioning kidneys to eliminate it. When she finally regained some of her thought process she had significant and permanent confusion a great deal of the time. She had become a shell of the sister I knew.

In May 2004, eight months after the hospital debacle, we sat at my kitchen table after she arrived for the weekend. I had been asked to share the heartbreaking news with her. The doctors said the dialysis wasn't working anymore. She had the option to continue but they had said her heart was so weak that the next heart attack (likely during dialysis since the process puts a strain on the heart) would be the end. I will remember, forever, the look in her eyes when she said, *"If I don't have the dialysis treatments then I'll die."* A lump formed in my throat and I steeled myself to go on. I told her that was true but that we didn't know when or how long she had left, only God knew. I couldn't cry. I had to hold it together at all costs and remain strong for her, my niece and my son. But inside I was already writhing with the pain of losing her in a matter of days. The look in her eyes to my youngest son and to me was from the depth of her soul. I can't explain it but I can tell you I saw her soul that day. I have never seen that depth in a person's eyes. The love radiating from her eyes combined with the fear she felt was overwhelming. I can close my eyes today and see that look. She died six days later. She had told me a few weeks before what she wanted me to include in her eulogy. She seemed to sense her time was close. She especially wanted me to end with, "See you later!" In my mind she was a human with issues just like we all have but to me she was my soul mate, my forever sister and forever friend. My son and I worked together on the eulogy. I related the story of her life and read a few song titles and lyrics while he played the accompanying music on the piano. Celine Dion's song, "I'm Your Angel," was especially fitting. Those beautiful words, "I'll be your power in the sky, your shoulder when you cry" summed up our relationship. I am so thankful that I can communicate with her to this day. I will always need her in my life.

What made our relationship so special? Well, my sister was the one person I could talk to if I was worried about something. After her humorous one-liners about the situation we would talk it through until it made sense. When we were lonely we would call each other and just hearing each other voice would cause things to look brighter and feel lighter as we laughed together through our fears. If I had good news or bad news she was the first one I wanted to share it with. She told me I was too serious, I told her someone had to be. When one of us read a good book, we would call the other to recommend it and tantalize them with the high points. More often than not the other person had just finished it. We just loved being together and could find humor or fun in the dumbest things. In the 1970s we both got identical afros and wore them with pride as we went for our appointments to a man who drew a picture of our own, individual spiritual guides. Later that day, sitting by the lake at my sister's house we thought a picture of the experience would be great. I still have the picture of us proudly holding up our spirit guide pictures and looking quite 'with it' with our new hair style. We had the same passion for just about everything including deep fried mushrooms and smoked fish. Most importantly we gave each other energy and loved each other, unconditionally. She was, and is, an essential part of my life and my best friend. Thanks kid, and yes, I will see you later; keep the gate open for me!

My son, mom and sister were always so important to me that it is not surprising that they refused to let me believe that they were totally gone after their death. We must have made some pact before entering this life that said none of us would be left alone. In the next chapter, I will explain the dream messages I received for two years from Ronnie. I have also transcribed some of the direct quotes from my recorded conversations I have had with Ronnie, my mom and sister over the last decade. I have the notes, cassette tapes and CDs dated and preserved. They are gifts to me from my loved ones. I have chosen to share selected parts of my communications, but not all. To share all the word-by-word messages could have resulted in me being 'banned from the tribe.' Seriously, the messages have been so direct, so pointed that I felt the need to reserve some of it in the archives of my mind.

Due to the evidence of this on-going connection, I know, unequivocally, that we truly are more than this mere physical body we inhabit. This is not simply a theory but has been demonstrated to me. We are not, most importantly, a body that has a spirit and soul but rather a spiritual being who has chosen to be in a physical form for a certain amount of time. When we leave our body, it is cast aside and our spirit and soul are free. Our loved ones' energy, which we know cannot be created nor destroyed — only changed in form, continues to exist and manifest itself in a different plane — a different vibrational level — of existence. They are no longer weighed down by the body or

73

heavy outer shell. Being from Michigan I relate it to taking off a heavy winter coat with a sweater underneath, together with your gloves, scarf, hat and boots. You feel so much lighter, right? If you could magnify this feeling a thousand-fold you could grasp the idea. Besides being lighter, our family on the other side is brighter. Our loved ones who have passed on are able to see, feel and know more than mere mortals. Why? Time and space are not the restrictive concepts for them as they are for us. They are ready to open the lines of communication with us. It is as if they are holding the other end of the phone in their hands and dialing our numbers, over and over, hoping we will pick up. They want to support and HELP. The unconditional love that we have for each other keeps us connected. It transcends all. It is the alpha and the omega, the beginning and the end, as we know it.

Again, I ask for those of you who are skeptical — please continue to be so while reading — but continue to read. To suspend one's belief is difficult, to leave one's comfort zone is often frightening; but to force yourself to continue to seek out new information into areas where you may never have been is courageous. My wish for you is that you will experience the peace in your head and heart that I have been able to attain by discovering that your loved ones are with you. Merely accepting this understanding as truth is healing for your heart. If you choose to go further and connect with them I know it is possible. Remember, you are never alone. In your darkest hour they are with you.

When we are meditating, or just about to fall asleep or wake up, our loved ones are closest to us. They are waiting patiently to reconnect. When you exhale the worries of the day and inhale the love that surrounds us from our loved ones, behind the door, those quiet visitors rush in to communicate and to help and touch our spirits. They want to let us know that we are safe and all is right with the world.

Part II

Conversations:
Sentiments, Observations and Opinions

PEOPLE LIKE US,
WHO BELIEVE IN PHYSICS, KNOW
THAT THE DISTINCTION BETWEEN
PAST, PRESENT AND FUTURE
IS ONLY A STUBBORNLY PERSISTENT
ILLUSION

Albert Einstein

I have received tremendous help from a wonderful woman named Lee who lives in Boulder, Colorado. I call her an angel on earth for many reasons. She is pure of heart, has a belief in a higher power and has been successful in opening the doors in my mind as well as the minds of hundreds and likely thousands of others. She has been so accurate that it has allowed me to suspend my disbelief, entertain the possibility and finally accept the help and love that my family on the other side have been eager to give. After she gently kicked me out of the nest, I now initiate the conversations with my loved ones directly. Thanks, Lee, for gently but firmly forcing me to do this for myself. It is indeed humbling and reassuring that they are so close. You were right all along!

Before meeting Lee and very soon after Ronnie passed, he seemed determined to get to me, and reassure me, that he was okay. I wanted you to know the type of person that he was so that you could understand that when he set his mind to something he never gave up. I understand now how his forceful personality refused to let me lock myself emotionally away from the world. I was into the grief process too deeply to be able to hear him myself; nor was I absolutely sure that this type of connection was even possible. I had read about it as a belief but never experienced it personally. Not to be put off, Ronnie connected with a close friend of mine who receives messages in his dreams. By his own choice I will not use his name. He is a devoted believer in a higher power and is the kind of person that you just know will have your best interest at heart. He is the type of person that is always willing to help someone out and will do whatever necessary to lend a hand. I admire him greatly and know that his gift allowed me, early in the grief process, to achieve the beginnings of not only a belief — but a true knowing — that Ronnie was always with me. It enabled me to momentarily lift the heaviness, the darkness that surrounded me, take a deeper breath and achieve a peace in my heart. My friend gave me a confirmation in my mind that I had not ever thought possible. He gave me hope when I needed it the most.

Thank you to both of these special individuals for helping me during the darkest period of my life. I know you are both motivated one hundred percent by love and have an unquestionable sense in a higher power. You actually made real for me what I had merely studied about since the early 1970s. I know what I have experienced and it is truth. I will continue to be a believer who learns daily and tries to help others realize there is so much more behind the door. Peace is eventually possible in both your head and heart after the death of a loved one. You will always miss them but you are able to move on with your life lessons. You will actually be able to breath normally again, taking in oxygen, the life force, in a regular manner rather than the short shallow breaths of someone who is hurting emotionally.

The first communication with my son through my friend mentioned above as a conduit started five months after Ronnie's passing and continued for two years. Now, I can hear him myself and no longer need a conduit. I have kept the records of these communications for two purposes. First, it has been a visual reminder that he is always nearby. Secondly, I knew that when the time was right, I would be able to help others develop a sense of peace and hope as their loved ones crossed to the other side. I know this communication is possible for anyone if they are motivated by unconditional love.

Dreams Relay Messages from the Other Side

In mid October 1999, just five months after Ronnie's death, my close friend came to me and said he occasionally had dreams that contained messages for people. He shared them if he believed that the people were receptive. I knew he had this gift but had not experienced it personally. He reiterated the following, which I quickly wrote down.

Ronnie had come to him during the night and told him to give me this message, "*I'm okay, Mom. I didn't feel any pain when I was killed.*" He said he was, "*At first confused and upset. I didn't think that I would be alive after I passed.*" Ronnie went on to tell me, "*Not to be so sad; we would all be together later.*" He continued by saying that he, "*Felt guilty abandoning us but wanted me to know about this place.*" He added, "*I wouldn't have left all of you for the world. I am afraid that you will forget me.*" He explained, "*I have been here with you and trying to help.*" He remarked that he, "*Felt responsible that I was so sad.*" My friend added that Ronnie had tears in his eyes when he was saying these things to him. Ronnie continued, "*We are in such grief that we can't see each other.*" He wanted me to know that

Grandma (my mother), *"Would die peacefully in her sleep and that it would be like a vigil for two to three days."* He advised me to, *"Talk with her and give her permission to go in peace."* As I thought about this it made sense. My mom was two months away from her ninety-first birthday and didn't seem to be interested in any type of celebration. I knew she would not leave this earth until she felt I had gotten through the toughest part of losing my son. Ronnie elaborated, *"The candles in her room will go out when she passes."* He ended by reiterating, *"Everything was as it should be and it was all meant to be."*

You can imagine my relief and joy to hear this message from my son. All of these emotions were suddenly hitting me. I was so relieved to hear something. I had read about souls transitioning to the other side but until this very moment my heart was still so heavy that I just could not internalize it. Ronnie let me know that he felt my sadness and his death was, *"All as it should be."* My head and my heart began to process the immensity of this message. I had not "lost" my son! He was with me now and always.

I needed to know more about all of this so I started reading about dreams. I learned that when we are in a dream state it is easier for the other side to communicate with us. Our normal activities, thoughts or worries are put on hold as we sleep. Basically, our vibrational level changes and allows our loved ones on the other side to get through the wall of grief we may have surrounding us. It began to make sense to me and helped me more fully understand the dream I had myself a few weeks previously.

To this point my one and only dream of Ronnie, had occurred three months after he died in August 1999. It was the most vivid dream I have ever experienced before or since that time. I remember going back to bed after getting up briefly about 4:00 AM. The dream occurred between 4:00 AM and 6:00 AM. I was so affected by it that I had to record it. I didn't know why at the time, I just knew I needed to make a point of remembering absolutely everything about it.

In the dream I was with Ronnie. I could feel his physical presence standing next to me — the big, macho guy that he was. We were observing the different businesses of his in Colorado, walking in and out of many single-story buildings. He was basically checking on how things were going. There were so many people around, adults as well as children. They were not family members but were customers and employees. They kept asking questions and seeking directions from him on what seemed to be a million different things.

I remember feeling frazzled in that environment. It seemed like he did not have a second to himself before the next person would come to him for something. For some reason I hadn't even been able to do my hair or put my makeup on that morning (something I had always done before starting the day). Everything was just so busy. It seemed like organized chaos to me. This was so much like the way Ronnie's businesses normally ran that he was used to it.

Ronnie then said to me, "*Mom, come on, I want to show you something.*" I said, "*Oh, Ronnie, I'm not dressed for the day.*" He brushed off my comment and said, "*It doesn't matter Mom, just come on.*" Off we went. We started walking a little ways and arrived at a rather unique, older home with such character. It had been turned into a boutique. It was rather strange in a way. It reminded me of a tree house since it seemed at least 20 feet off the ground. We had to go up some kind of spiral steps to get into the home. But instead of him helping me up the steps, he had built some kind of lift on the platform to get up to the door. I remember thinking once I was up there, how ingenious he was to have a way to get into the house without going up all those stairs. I definitely remember the feeling of going up. He was standing next to me and opened the door for me to enter.

On the inside of the door, there was an inscription in cursive writing on the brass doorknob that looked like it had been scratched into the metal. It took my breath away and tears formed in my eyes. It read, "To the people that move into this home, it was a very loving home. My children and I enjoyed it very much. We loved to be here until the death of their father, my husband." I was so saddened by reading it and looked at Ronnie and said, "*Oh, look at this,*" as tears streamed down my face. He said, "*Mom, it will be okay, just let it go.*"

At that point, he gently placed his hands on my shoulders and turned me around to see the room. It was filled with the most gorgeous,

short-length women's jackets I had ever seen! They were displayed
on all of the walls of the room and hanging on racks. There were so
many of them and the colors were so vibrant that they were absolutely
mesmerizing. The only way I can describe the colors is 'other world-
like.' I lack the words to adequately describe the beauty in these pieces.
The reds, yellows, greens, blues and browns were not just the colors we
see on earth but seem to radiate light from inside the individual threads
of the fabric. I can close my eyes today and see those magnificent,
breathtaking pieces. In addition to the materials you normally see in
unique jacket designs there were brocades, and leathers with unusual
lace trimming, pearls sewn into the fabrics and flashy stones woven
into many of the individual pieces. The decorative designs and unusual
placement of trim pieces seemed to make each jacket more outstanding
than the one before it. Each was definitely one-of-a-kind. I recall
thinking, where would you ever wear one of these incredible pieces? I
didn't think I could even afford to buy one. You could tell only the best
designers and most exquisite tailors had been involved in their creation.
Then I thought what a tremendous investment of time and money had
gone into creating this unusual boutique. I looked up at my son in awe.
All I could say was *"Ronnie!"* He gave me a big smile and said *"Come
on, I've got to show you something else."*

We walked across a hall to the left and into the next room about the
same size, 40 X 40. It was another boutique but this one was designed
around a Christmas theme. The happy, joyous feelings of Christmas and
fresh pine scent filled the air as we walked in. Beautiful Christmas music
with harps and French horns played in the background. There were
so many unusual decorations for Christmas trees and other Christmas
décor for the house. The colors, once again, were 'other world like.'
The items seem to radiate the colors from within. A rainbow would
pale by comparison. How would you ever choose which one to buy?
As I looked around each one was stunning and seemingly more unique
than the one before it. It was hard to take it all in. The little music boxes
with winter themes painted on them rang out the melodic sounds of
Christmas carols. The wind chimes even seemed to ring out in tones
that reflected the joyous season. The colors were so brilliant that you

just wanted to stop and absorb them into your very being. It was the most peaceful and happy place that I had ever seen. He looked at me and said, *"Well, what do you think?"* I was speechless at this point and could only manage to say, *"Oh, Ronnie."* I was going to add, *"Honey, this is incredible but how can you take on more businesses?"* I felt it would just be too much, too overwhelming to keep yet more business ventures going. His eyes were sparkling and he laughed as he said, *"You're son's not so dumb after all is he?"* He had made this statement before when he was alive. Usually it had followed a good financial deal — a profit — that he had just made when buying or selling something. I would just shake my head and laugh. I always gave him the same reply, *"There's nothing dumb about you at all! You have the Midas touch!"*

The dream was just ending as I was waking, I remember having to lie in bed for at least ten minutes. I was so overcome by all of it that I couldn't even move — actually didn't want to move. I just wanted to bask in the feelings of joy and love that I was having at that moment. I felt that I had actually been with my son. As I was getting ready for work the overwhelming feeling of happiness remained. A part of me was in total awe at what I had just seen. Was it real? No one else had experienced it. How I wished someone else could have witnessed it so that I would know I wasn't just making this stuff up in my mind in a desperate need to hold on to him. The dream was so real it felt like I had stepped into a perfectly staged movie scene with Ronnie. I didn't want to leave.

He had picked two of my absolute favorite things to this day — unusual, fun and dramatic jackets and Christmas decorations to relay the message of moving on with peace and grace. I had never before nor since had a dream like that one. It seemed so real and in living color no less! To this day, I have had only one dream in color in my life and this was it. I understand some people do dream in color. I guess I'm just too much of a black and white person to achieve the color thing. My son had found a way to get a message through to me even in my grief. He used the dream state as a necessity. I was so emotionally blocked from my grief that nothing was really going in or out. The doors in my mind were not only closed but firmly locked! My son refused to let me stay in this state and found a way to get to me when I wasn't looking! Ultimately as I reflected back to the experience, I wasn't too surprised that he had found me even in my dream state. Ronnie could always find me even if I was on a trip and gone from my school district in Michigan. If I was at an educator's conference it was not uncommon for the phone to ring at 8:30 A.M. It would be Ronnie, from Colorado, just checking to see how I was doing. The statement you can run but you can't hide was his theme song.

Mom Knew When She Would Be Moving On

My mom taught me how to be a mother. She sacrificed everything for her kids. She always wanted more for her girls than she had. Her favorite saying was, *"Blood is thicker than water."* When it came to being there for us, she was number one. She could also stop you in your tracks with 'her look' if she wanted to get your attention. My dad had emigrated from England with his family when he was seventeen-years old. He looked just like a movie star, had a British accent and drove a new car. He was too much for my mom to pass up. At twenty-years old she broke off her engagement to a dentist and married my dad after a short courtship. Although Dad always lived with us, my mom was the parent that I admired tremendously, feared a little and loved the most.

She was brilliant and had won a scholarship to go to business school, which was quite remarkable for a girl in 1925. Sadly, she couldn't take advantage of it since she had to drop out in her senior year of high school to help support her family when her father was dying of black lung disease. She was meticulous about her appearance and had a fashion sense that simply worked even on a limited budget. She knew about 'foundation garments' and worked for a women's store that specialized in them. I remember when the owner of the store offered her the position of buyer she was so honored. Twice a year she would have to travel to New York to review the latest designs and decide on the lines to be purchased for the store's inventory. My dad would not even consider letting her take the advancement. Without complaint she continued in her existing position and upheld her belief that it was nearly a crime if anything moved or jiggled on your body once you were dressed! Bright red nail polish was her signature look and seemed perfect for her delicate, feminine hands. She thought the clear nail polish I always wore left much to be desired. At eighty-nine-years of age she made a radical decision and told me that I didn't need to color her massive head of hair anymore. As it grew out it was a soft white that seemed even more perfect for her skin tone than the blonde shade we had been using for years. She was a lady in every sense of the word.

With all of her strengths she remained, however, fearful about life, about being alone just like my sister. She could never understand why I was not afraid to do all the traveling I had to do for my job. Or why I would take on additional job opportunities and challenges. Of course, she lived through the Depression era, which affected many people's sense of security and well-being. Her perspective was "a bird in the hand is worth two in the bush." Conversely, my perspective has always been, "If there's a pile there must be a pony in it somewhere." Although we differed greatly in our views of "opportunities" in life we loved each other deeply. There was definitely a special bond between us.

About two months after Ronnie died my mom who was ninety-years old came to live with us permanently rather than just visiting on weekends. Since she had lost her first born, a son named Vincent (Vinny) when he was a year and one half, she understood about losing a child. I remember she would always comment around October 14th that Vinny would have been such and such age today. She made a point of commenting about his birthdate for sixty-seven years. She was just twenty-three-years old when he died. Although there was rarely twenty-five cents to spare after the bills were paid she somehow managed to have a picture of the two of them taken by a professional photographer. This would have been a very bold move for my mom. The portrait appears to have been taken about three months before his death from scarlet fever. I still have the picture and looking at it you can see how her gentle eyes just radiated the love and pride she felt for him. He was definitely her pride and joy. Ten months after Vinny's death, in 1933, Mom and Dad had twin girls. My mom told me later that my dad and his family thought the best way for her to get over Vinny's death was to have another child as soon as possible. She never had the time to truly work through her grief of losing her son before her hands were full raising identical twin girls. Their marriage was one of endless bickering and turmoil. Mom described it as trying to mix oil and water. The only thing they seemed to have in common was their initial physical attraction to each other and the children. Dad had received his draft papers in late 1944 and went off to the Navy. My sisters and mom moved in with my grandmother and I was born a few months later. Mom was a wonderful parent who was fiercely protective of her offspring. She was highly opinionated and brutally honest. When you combined these traits with her dry sense of humor it resulted in occasional comments that could shock an innocent observer. She would come up with one liner's that caused me to laugh until tears rolled down my cheeks. My Mom and sister shared the same sense of humor.

In August 1999, she had come to live with us permanently. She was in a wheelchair due to severe arthritis in her knees. Her mind, however, remained as sharp as a tack! She didn't really take medication other than one pill a day for arthritis. No problems with blood pressure, cholesterol or heart. Other than using hearing aides (which she wore but purposely turned off when Dad was alive), she was in great shape. In fact, I couldn't even get her to take vitamins. She thought they might "interfere" with her arthritis medication! She was amazingly healthy for over ninety-years of age.

In September, she was sitting at the kitchen table and looked out over our backyard in Michigan. It was rimmed with trees and had two large oak trees near the center. She pointed to one tree, closest to the deck and kitchen window and said, *"Mary, when the last leaf on that tree falls, I will be leaving this earth."* This was not only a shock to hear but especially difficult to accept since Ronnie's death had only been four months before. I discounted it and said, *"Oh Mom, don't talk that way, you are fine."* Nonetheless at least once a week she would repeat this statement and, in turn, I would give her the same response. I had taken her to get a physical in August and the doctor said she was fine. I refused to believe that she was getting ready to leave.

Seeking advice, I mentioned Mom's comment to a board of education member who was a nurse and good friend. She asked to come by and see mom a few days later. I said. *"Sure, Mom likes to have company."* I made myself scarce and went to another part of the house so they could visit. When the visit was over I walked my friend to her car and she said, *"Mary, I think we need to contact Hospice."* I was astounded. *"Hospice,"* I said, *"Why would we do that? Isn't Hospice for someone who is dying? Mom is fine, she is just like she has always been except in a wheelchair now."* My friend was so patient and gentle and just put her hand on my arm and said, *"I will contact them for you."*

The next thing I knew Hospice was a part of our lives. Mom seemed to respond well to them. They were absolutely a godsend. They decided about one month later that she needed oxygen when she slept at night. She even requested and received a visit from the parish priest. Everything was done with such personal privacy and dignity for her. She was the decision maker and remained so during the three months they came to see her. After work one night, I walked into her room and saw some paperwork on the bureau. It was a DNR order. I didn't even know what it meant until I read it. Sure enough, Mom's signature was on the bottom! I decided not to say anything then but to wait until the weekend when we had more time to talk. The next Saturday as I was doing her hair I said to her, "Mom is it time to say good bye to me." She indignantly replied, "I will NEVER be ready to say good bye to you." End of story! My mom was a lady of few words and she meant every one of them. I just seemed to be watching this play being acted out in front of me with all the needed preparations and in such a classy manner but couldn't seem to get Mom to talk to me about it. The lyrics from Celine Dion's song, "Goodbye's (The Saddest Word)" best describes our relationship, "There is no other love like a mother's love for her child…"

Reflecting back, I feel she willed herself to stay on earth for six months after Ronnie's death to be sure I would be okay. Saying good bye would have been too hard for either of us to do so her weekly statement, "*When the last leaf is off that tree, I will be gone,*" would have to suffice. No discussion, no drama, just the sentence repeated as a gentle reminder.

On the evening of November 16th, I had hurried home from work so that we could take mom the forty miles into Kalamazoo to see my sister, Phyllis, who was in the hospital. Not wanting to take the time to make dinner, I suggested that we stop at Arby's and get some sandwiches to eat in the car. My husband and younger son were in the front seat and I was sitting in back with Mom. I had unwrapped her sandwich and noticed she hadn't even taken a bite. I asked her what was wrong and she said quietly, "*Mary, I don't think I can hold it.*" Although I was surprised by her response, I told her that wasn't a problem and I would hold it for her. Mom hadn't ever acted this way. I held the sandwich so she could take a bite. She took a small bite and as she tried to swallow it she coughed and said in a whisper, "*The pain, Mary.*" I asked her where the pain was located and she motioned with her right hand to her chest, left arm and said it hurt in her back also. I gave her an aspirin and told my husband and son that we better turn the car around and go home and get Mom into bed and on her oxygen. It was six months to the day that Ronnie had been killed when Mom had her chest pains. She was never a complainer so when she acted this way I knew it was serious. I asked her if she wanted me to call Hospice and she said no, it wasn't necessary. I assumed she meant that after a good night's sleep she would be better. As I was getting Mom into bed, the irony of having her experience the heart pains on this date made it even more difficult to accept.

The next morning she was awake when I went in to check on her. Since she hadn't eaten the night before, I was going to make her some tea and toast and take it to her room before Daisy, Mom's day care provider, arrived. I asked her if that sounded good and she said, "*Honey, I think I would rather have a shot.*" Confused I said a shot of what?

89

Mom replied, "*Whiskey, and would you sit with me while I drink it?*" It was 7:00 AM and Mom rarely indulged, maybe a whiskey sour ever six months. She told me she wanted the shot for "medicinal purposes" as people of her generation referred to it. I took the shot glass back to her and just sat in the chair next to her bed and talked with her. I had called into work and said I would be late. I didn't want to hurry or have Mom think that I wouldn't take the time she wanted and needed from me. She must have sipped that small shot of whiskey for an hour as we talked. As I recall we talk about everything and nothing at the same time. What we didn't talk about was anything to do with her death. We talked about Ronnie, Vinny, my two sisters who were both alive at the time and the beautiful sunny November day. It was just a regular mother-daughter talk. She was feeling a little tired then and I just had a feeling that I needed to be close to her for the rest of the day. So I made a second call to work and told them I needed to stay home for the day. When Daisy arrived to sit with Mom, I decided to take a shower. As I was cleaning up I heard a peal of laughter coming from Daisy and I threw a robe around me and hurried into the bedroom. Mom needed to use the commode in her room and asked Daisy to help her. As Daisy wrapped her arms around Mom from the back to guide her over to the seat, Mom commented to Daisy, tongue-in-cheek, "*We've got to stop meeting like this!*" Tears of laughter were running down Daisy's cheeks. Regardless of her age, mom's quick wit frequently caught people off guard. Nothing passed by her radar!

It was too hard to believe 'she was on her way out.' For the following forty-eight hours, the Hospice nurse and social worker came by to check her. She just continued to sleep through it and gradually became unresponsive. Toward the evening of the second day, mom started the heavy labored breathing. I now know through my Hospice training that it is an indicator of the patient being in the active stage of dying. At the time, however, I just wanted to get rid of what sounded like congestion in her chest. I thought she must be uncomfortable. I climbed up into her bed and held her as I rested her back against my chest. Nothing worked. When the Hospice team stopped by again later that evening they explained that it was a natural part of the process and that mom was not uncomfortable. They must be right, I thought, since there hadn't been any grimaces or indicators of pain on her face. Still, I just wanted to do something to stop the sound — the reminder — that Mom was getting ready to leave. During the previous twelve hours or so, Mom's mouth became firmly closed as she slept. The best that could be done was to soak a small sponge swab in water to wet her lips. I had made the calls to my sisters and soon the whole family, my sisters, nieces and spouses were camped out at the house. Friends stopped in for short visits and I just stayed in the room with Mom. About 3:00 A.M., November 19, 1999, Mom stopped that loud, rattle sound in her breathing and started to breath normally — or so I thought. I remember thinking, good she is getting better! She had not moved a muscle during the previous forty-eight hours. She was resting comfortably due to the vigilance of the Hospice workers and I now know that she was doing her own mental and emotional work in preparation to pass on. I was sitting on the floor next to her bed and my eleven-year-old son was with me, asleep in a lounge chair in her room. All of a sudden, he was fully awake, bolted out of the chair, and came around the back of me to put his hands on my shoulders. I instinctively looked up at Mom. She moved her head to look upward and to the right. She did not open her eyes but furrowed her brow and moved her head back down. About three seconds later she moved her head up again and to the right, this time, without furrowed brow and took her last breath. Obviously, she wanted to be sure of what she was 'seeing.' I had a candle burning in the room and it went out as Ronnie said it would. Both of my boys were with me to give me support, just in different ways.

I absolutely know my Mom saw the other side. Vinny, her first born, was probably there to help her across and at first she couldn't believe it, hence the furrowed brow. Being a cautious person, she looked a second time to be sure of what she was seeing and then was ready to make her journey.

As Hospice had promised they had been there, on and off, throughout the forty-eight-hour vigil. They did everything possible to make sure Mom was comfortable and I was aware of what was happening. They were a true gift from heaven.

When I called the priest to come over to see mom two days before, he said, "*Mary, I have already been there to give her Absolution.*" All this was not something Mom chose to share with me. I guess the finality of it was too hard to discuss. I also believe she felt that this was not the end but a change in venue. I know for sure, the second time she moved her head, just before her last breath, she had a glimpse of the other side and was ready to move on. She passed quietly with dignity just as she lived. I looked at her face and her skin was as taunt as a thirty-year old. Other family members who walked into her room after her death commented on it as well. Mom would mention her displeasure about her wrinkles from time to time. She detested them and refused to believe that at ninety-years old they added character to her face. As the door opened to the other side she decided to leave her wrinkles behind. Well done, Mom!

I woke up my two sisters up so they could each have time alone with Mom before I called the funeral home. I walked outside to get a breath of fresh air. At that point I had been up for two days and was functioning on autopilot. As I walked into the back yard I looked up at the tree, and the leaf was gone! It had been hanging on the limb a few hours before when I had taken a quick five-minute break. Where was it? The wind, so common in the Michigan winters, had literally blown away all the leaves from the trees. As the outside lights illuminated the yard, only one leaf remained. There it was, right at the bottom of the tree about two feet from the trunk. I picked it up and brought it into the house and said to my sisters, "*Hey, guys, Mom was right, when the last leaf was off the tree she would be gone.*" True to form we all shed a few tears and Phyllis made a wise crack and we laughed. Mom would have wanted it to be handled just that way. My mother was 99.9 percent right about everything in her life and ours. It was fitting to recognize that she, indeed, was right about her time of death. I had the leaf encased in hard plastic and have it to this day. My mom, just as my son had done, out of love and concern, gave me a message to get prepared since they would be leaving this earth plane.

It is amazing how little most of us really know about the precarious balance between life and death. How humbled we can become when we experience how unconditional love can transcend time and circumstance. I realize now how fortunate I was to be able to receive these messages before their deaths. How did they know? Again, is it the subconscious speaking through them? Is it God, the Universe, or whatever you choose to call a higher power that helps you to prepare yourself and your loved ones for the moment of death in which you will no longer inhabit a physical body? I don't know for sure what it is but I do know it exists because my loved ones have demonstrated it to me.

I do not believe that there is death of the totality of who we are, simply death of one rather insignificant part, the outer shell. Our spirit and soul lives on. It is the true essence of who we are for eternity. I also know that it is the unconditional love and openness to the other side that allows us to continue our conversations for as long as we choose. Energy cannot be created nor destroyed only changed in form.

Beef Tongue, Lemon Curd and Waterfalls

O n the first weekend in May 2000, nearing the first anniversary of
Ronnie's death, I was home and had been continually thinking
about Ronnie. I thought sadly, 'No more Mother's Day flowers or cards
from him.' The year before I had received a beautiful bouquet of roses
with a loving note from Ronnie and Gina. They arrived on Saturday,
May 15th, the day before he was killed. The thought of Mother's Day
without him made my heart ache.

I thought I had worked through the stages of loss that Dr. Elisabeth
Kübler-Ross had written about, and I had to a certain degree. But I
seemed to have this yearning to hear from him from time to time and
be assured, yet again, that he was okay— that he was somewhere — and
that he hadn't just disappeared into the cosmos. My head told me he was
still around but my heart, being especially tender during this particular
week, needed relief from the melancholy I was feeling. When you are
in grief the assurances you receive are never quite enough. You always
want just one more.

I believe most mothers want to know that our kids are healthy and, of course, eating right. Well, for me this extended to the other side as well. Ronnie was easy to cook for and I had always tried to make sure that he ate good meals. My friend, the dream messenger, who had been chosen by Ronnie to continue the connection with me since I still couldn't do it for myself, didn't have any respite from our constant need to reconnect. I was, however, a bit surprised to see him at my door this particular Mother's Day weekend. As soon as I opened it he said, *"I had a dream again and Ronnie wanted you to know that he is eating beef tongue!"* When he said it, I thought he was going to choke. He explained that he had never eaten it and hopefully never would. Obviously, he did not know that one of the things Ronnie and I shared a passion for was beef tongue. It was truly our favorite meat! We had acquired the taste from my dad who was raised with it in Tamworth, England. The rest of the family would not consider eating it! The only time I even cooked it was when Ronnie was coming over. I knew Ronnie's ingenuous Mother's Day message was meant to assure me, once again, that he was okay and not to continue to worry. I needed to hear this. It made Mother's Day a little easier.

The following week I was thinking about my mom. Since she and I had always been so close and Ronnie seemed to be able to get through to me, I wondered to myself, 'Why isn't Mom trying to get to me at least to tell me she is okay?' Two days after thinking about Mom, my friend, once again, came to see me. He handed me a jar of Lemon Curd.

For those of you who are unfamiliar, it is a sweet topping that can be put on toast. It is rather like a thick jelly made primarily of lemons. It is a favorite of the British. Mom had always loved it. When she was living with us I made sure to have an ample supply in the pantry. When my friend handed me the jar he said, "I had to go to three stores this weekend to find this. I have never eaten it but it is from your mom. She told me in my dream to tell you to, *"Give yourself a little treat!"* You may have guessed it, lemon curd or lemon cheese as it had been called when my British grandmother used to make it was also one of the favorite things that Mom and I had in common! I just thought to myself, 'Thanks Mom, I just needed to hear from you and know you are fine.'

During the spring in 2004, this same friend came to see me again. He said he had another dream about Ronnie. He said that Ronnie was concerned. One of his twins was having difficulty with a boy from school. It seemed that this boy's father was well connected in the school environment. He also gave me the name of this boy. He told me to contact Gina and ask her about it and then tell her not to go to school and make a big deal out of it. He said part of the issue was that this boy was always talking about his dad and Ronnie's son felt empty inside since he had lost his dad. He then added something else that surprised us. He said that this son could actually hear Ronnie speak to him. He needed to be told that he truly was hearing his dad, that it was real.

I called Gina and asked how the boys were doing. She said one of the twins was having trouble at school with another boy. I asked if his name was ... She said, "Yes!" I told her about the message I had received from Ronnie. The next time I had the chance to talk to my grandson directly I asked him if he heard his dad talking to him at times and he confirmed that he did. I assured him that it was real and not to think that there was anything wrong with him. I went on to explain that not everyone can hear these things so it might be better just to keep it to himself or to talk to his mom or me about it if he wanted to. He seemed to appreciate our talk and I told him it was a gift to be able to hear our loved ones who have passed on.

Children are open vessels of trust and love. Many times, when they are young, they are more receptive and are able to receive messages that adults cannot. They have not yet been programmed to think it can't happen Isn't it interesting that as adults, we need to relearn what the youngest among us already know? How beautiful it is to realize that the other side can make this connection with them. Maybe invisible playmates are not simply made up in a child's imagination after all!

In April 2005, my friend came to me again and said he had another dream. This time he said it was kind of funny to begin with. He said Ronnie literally woke him up and told him to, *"Get a piece of paper and write down what I am going to say."* Ronnie went on to say, *"Ma likes to hear it exact!"* I had been concerned with a family situation regarding Gina and didn't want to overstep my bounds as a mother-in-law. Ronnie assured me that what was happening was okay and that it would work at this point in her life. He ended by saying, *"Mom, I know you guys have been there for the boys and you always will be. And I love you and my brother for that — Ma — it's okay."*

There were other messages I received through my friend from Ronnie about my work environment. I have chosen not to include them for many reasons. Suffice it to say, when the going got rough, as is frequently the case in any large educational institution, Ronnie always came through with such candor and offered me "his two cents" as he put it. These messages were spot on regarding the challenges of the moment. They were very descriptive of what my challenge was and all ended with ideas and words of encouragement in tackling the latest issue. Since his death he has continued to watch out for me just as he did when he was alive. He still seems bigger-than-life to me but now I know why — because he is!

For the remaining eight years I was in the district, just when I was facing a major dilemma or was quite concerned about something, Ronnie would find a way to get through to me. I never relied on it but was always thankful to hear from him. I knew my son was keeping an eye on me from his unique vantage point. He had twenty-twenty hindsight, present-sight and future-sight. Ronnie had not, after all, simply disappeared into the cosmos! But had continued to be an integral part of my life.

In April 2001, I had another unusual experience. My friend came to deliver the latest message. Ronnie said, *"Mom, everything is going to be all right, you need to trust your instincts but you need to take it easy. You can't carry everything on your shoulders. I will be with you on your vacation watching the waterfalls and going up the stairs with you. Ma, I love you and I know you will do the right thing."* He went on to say, *"Thank you, Gina, for taking care of our boys and thank you for letting Ma be a part of your life. You need to go on with your life. I love you and I will always look after you."*

When I received this message from my friend our vacation plans had been set for months. We had waited two years to exchange our timeshare week for a place on the Kona coast in Hawaii. We had a great time that week and visited many places on the island. All the time I kept waiting to see the waterfalls and steps that Ronnie had mentioned. Since the weather had been rainy for three days that week some excursions that we had planned had to be cancelled. I thought that in cancelling one of them I must have missed the waterfalls and stairs. On the last night we decided, at the last minute, to go all out and have dinner at an upscale restaurant. Actually the hotel we drove to was so huge it had nine different restaurants in it. The inside décor was absolutely exquisite. After we decided on a particular restaurant we made reservations and they apologetically told us that there was an hour or so wait. No problem, we had the time to investigate the inside of the hotel and enjoy the manicured grounds. Inside and out, every architectural detail of the structure was built to perfection. It even had a waterway inside with small boats to take you to the different restaurants or shopping areas. We continued walking and enjoying the numerous pieces of art throughout the inside hallways next to the 'river' as the boats passed by. We decided to walk down to the dolphin pool which was close to the ocean. That was something I had thought we might have enjoyed, swimming with the dolphins. By the time I looked into it, it was too late to get reservations. We asked for directions at the concierge desk. Okay, easy enough to find. As we were climbing the two flights of stairs, I had this overwhelming feeling of peace come over me. I was remarking how beautiful and serene everything was that evening. The smells, colors and lighting all seemed to meld together to create the perfect ambience. Imagine my surprise when we came to the top of the stairs and directly across from us on a small island about 30 yards away, was the most beautiful waterfall — actually three waterfalls, each cascading into the other! I knew then that Ronnie was with me. It took my breath away and I said a little prayer of thanks to Ronnie and the Universe while my younger son and I had our picture taken on the top stairs with the falls behind us. Our plans to eat at this hotel and specific restaurant didn't even materialize until two hours before, yet Ronnie had explicitly described the setting two weeks prior.

Returning to Michigan, my friend asked me if I had experienced the three waterfalls and stairs that were a sign that Ronnie was with me. I told him the story. He seemed stunned by my explanation of our trip. He looked at me with a puzzled look in his eyes and said, *"You went where? I thought you were going to Florida!"* Since he had been to Florida many times he added, *"I couldn't think any of anyplace that resembled the place Ronnie told me about in my dream and was worried that I hadn't understood him in my dream but I passed it on to you anyway."*

Ronnie Explains His Death

In early January 2001 was the first time I met Lee in Boulder. She is one of the two people I mentioned earlier that helped me connect with my loved ones on the other side. Lee is a medium who has the incredible ability to remove the curtain that exists between our two worlds. This started my own direct communication with my family on the other side. My younger son, daughter-in-law and husband were all with me the first time we met. We had decided to go for a family reading since we were still in grief from the loss of Ronnie. Lee is truly the happiest person I have ever met. She radiates a peace and gentleness about her that is beyond description. She is a petite woman with an angel's voice. To me she is just a gift from heaven. I believe she was sent here to help us understand the depth and power of communication with the other side through unconditional love.

I realize that you may not be ready to wrap your head around the experiences I am going to share with you. That is understandable. There is a saying in spiritualism that when the student is ready, the teacher comes along. We have to be ready to move out of our comfort zone and suspend our existing belief system long enough to experience something new. For those who are ready, I pray that sharing the following experiences with you will be the little push you need to attain a greater sense of peace and possibly seek more answers for yourself. Your family members on the other side are patiently waiting.

I know I was not prepared that day for what I heard. I believe we were all in shock by the specifics she was able to give us. To begin, Lee started laughing and said, "Your son has quite a sense of humor." Anyone who knew Ronnie knew his wicked sense of humor was his trademark. She went on to say, Ronnie says to tell you " *I love you and I am fine.*" He says, *"I'm sorry, I didn't know it was going to happen."* He added, *"It was a shock to me too."* (I had been wondering if he had experienced a premonition about his death since our conversation in his truck a few weeks before he was killed.) I also wondered if he had suffered since it was such a traumatic accident. Ronnie said, *"No, I did not suffer but was a little confused when it happened."* He went on to say that he, *"Had been greeted by an older male"* in his transition. He told me that he, *"Couldn't have stayed on this earth after the accident or he would have been a vegetable."* He continued by saying that he, *"Saw Gina working on him but couldn't come back."* He said, *"Being here isn't painful, I'm nurtured, completely sustained."* He added, *"Mom you hear me talking to you."* I had thoughts come to me that sounded like Ronnie but I didn't know if my mind was simply playing tricks on me. He said again, *"I love you Mom. I'm okay."* He went on to say, *"I know where to find you!"* He said he was, *"Learning a great deal and it was like being at a university."* He also said, *"You and I will be together for eternity."* He told me he was, *"Always with me even though I couldn't see him."* He reminded me, *"To lighten up."* He added, *"I am so sorry that I had to leave but I am okay."* I did ask him if he woke my younger son up, out of that deep sleep in the recliner, to come over and put his hands on my shoulders when my Mom was about to take her last breath. He said, *"Yes, Mom I did that, we both needed to be there with you."*

When he communicated with Gina through Lee he called her "Babe." This was a nickname that he had given her early in their relationship. He said she was, *"Doing a good job with the boys."* And that he, *"Wished that I could give you a million dollars."* He said he, *"Had someone picked out for her down the road and that she shouldn't be alone.*" He jokingly added that she, "*Needed someone with all his 'good" qualities'!*" He told her not to worry that he has selective hearing at times and that, "*God knows I dumped enough.*" He assured her he was, "*Always around you as well and that you would know it from different signs*" that he would give her. He added that he, "*Loved her and the boys so much and that someone in the future would come into her life to help her.*" He added, "*You need people around you and you should decide where you want to live.*" This seemed to be a confirmation from him that wherever Gina wanted to live, Dolores, Denver or wherever would be fine. She had briefly thought about moving out of Dolores soon after his death but realized that he had always thought the small town would be the best place to raise the kids.

He went on and talked to his brother, my youngest son and said he was, "*Glad that you have found your talent this early and won't waste time like I did.*" He told him that he would, "*Travel and have many different teachers*" and added, "*I am glad you are so good in music. I love you.*" Ronnie ended by saying, "*Thanks for taking care of Mom. She's a handful!*"

Mom came into the session next. She had passed on six months after Ronnie was killed and five years after my Dad died. They had been married over sixty-four years and it had been a tumultuous marriage; I wondered how they were doing on the other side. Mom said that Dad had handed her a flower and that, "*It's okay, I took it.*" She added, "*We should have been born as brother and sister, it would have been much better. I loved him but didn't particularly like him.*" She ended by saying, "*He's at a different place of learning than I am but I check on him from time to time.*"

The session went on for well over an hour. In addition to the messages, I kept thinking about the language and vocabulary that Lee had used. It sounded as though Ronnie was talking directly to me on the phone. He talked differently to me than to Gina, which made sense. I was so amazed and shocked that this was possible. When my mom came through, Lee also used her particular phrases, even her voice inflections. The difference was astounding between the conversations. I just kept thinking, it sounds like they are either on the phone or in the next room! I knew that they may be gone from us physically, but they were somewhere close by. They were answering questions through

Lee before I even had the chance to ask most of them! In fact, I had forgotten about the questions I had written beforehand and left them in my purse when our session began. I felt relieved to know that I could have contact with him when I wanted it through Lee. The previous dream messages I had received from my friend were so comforting but this approach allowed me to actually initiate a conversation. Ronnie ended by saying, *"You will be able to communicate with me directly as time goes on."*

When I left Lee that day I felt I had a new lease on life. I had such a peaceful feeling, one that I had not felt since Ronnie's death. I had been open to the thought that life goes on after death — maybe in a different form but the belief was simply a belief. Now I knew for certain. This was a life-changing moment for me. Life would never be quite the same again. I had confirmation that my son and Mom were doing well and were only a thought away from me at any moment. This second confirmation from a completely different source allowed me to attain the unconditional belief in my head and heart that our loved ones are with us after they pass on and want to help and guide us along as we attempt to learn our own life lessons.

After this session and more studying and discussions with other people, I finally understood that when you are still in the depths of grief you are not able to 'hear' the words or thoughts as they are sent to you. Our loved ones are trying so hard to get through to us but the wall of sadness blocks the connection. It is such a challenge, to get through the stages of grief and get to a place where you can reach out for help in making this connection with the other side. I promise you, however, once you do you will never be the same. Life will have meaning again!

I hurt for many people I have met even today. I can tell by the deep sadness in their eyes that they have lost a child or close loved one and have not been able to move on with their lives. They seem to be stuck in the denial, grief or anger stage and just can't let go. It has been said that to feel both hopeless and helpless is the most devastating emotional state to be in. It feels like we are on a rudderless boat, just floating through life, unable to regain direction and sense of purpose. Life is a series of changes and the loss of a loved one is the biggest change to accept. Some people remain in a frozen emotional state of denial. Any further life challenge especially involving loss that crops up just adds to their feelings of inadequacy, fear and abandonment.

Trust me, I am not saying I was the poster child for moving on! Even though I was working full time, for the first two years after Ronnie's death, when I was home, I read just about every book on losing a child I could get my hands on. Many people actually sent me books on the topic. My community members were so generous that at one point I had three copies of the same book about losing a son. It helped to read these stories. They were like a lifeline — a reassurance — that there were people out there who were able to make it through their grief and once again, could function. I remember thinking, they have survived the change, their loved one is no longer with them and they appear to have reached a resolution with their loss. It gave me hope when I needed it most.

The talented actor, Liam Neeson who lost his beautiful wife, Natasha Richardson in a skiing accident two years ago at Mont Tremblant Resort in Quebec said in an interview on TV, "Just when you think you are making progress a special day or memory hits you." When I heard this I knew all to well what he was saying. These moments bring you back to the, "Why did this have to happen" stage and subsequent feeling that life is so unfair. Grief does strange things to your mind. Sometimes you do not want to move on for fear that if you let go of the actual event of the death you will not have anything left. Often we hold on to the anger or disbelief or depression because in our minds it is better to have that than nothing at all. I understand completely. I lived it. However, these negative emotions will freeze-frame your life leaving you an empty vessel of what you once were. You will not be able to complete the life lessons you are on this earth to learn. When I realized that if I did not learn my lessons I may have to come back in my next life and do it all again, I realized that I had no choice but to move on. I couldn't think of a worse scenario than repeating a life that involved the constant loss of loved ones. I had to get it right this time.

Right after Ronnie was killed I could not believe the world was going on as normal. Didn't they know my son was gone? Didn't they care enough to stop their incessant chatter and regular schedules long enough to let me be alone with my thoughts? Well, I'm not sure in reflecting back if I would really call them thoughts. My mind was rather like a blank canvass. I could sit for any length of time and it seemed like nothing was going in and nothing was coming out. The only exception to this was when I was at work. The break-neck pace needed in my job was an escape. I would be totally involved working on the district's needs until I got into my car at the end of the day and the reality of the loss would hit me. Tears would flow down my checks as I drove the ten minutes to the house.

I have read that when a person is in an accident and the physical pain is too intense the brain kicks in to protect the person from actually feeling or remembering the pain. I believe that is what happens to our minds when our grief is so overwhelming. It seems to shut down certain emotions or at least short circuits them until you are able to bear the immensity of the loss and the unbearable heaviness in your heart. Some people remain in this state of existence for years, not living, just merely existing. The most painful time for me was the first ten seconds upon waking in the morning. At first I would feel somewhat normal until I remembered what had happened and then this wave of sadness and nausea engulfed me. I would tear up and think, "Please God, give me the strength to get through another day without him."

Ronnie played football for eight years, and loved it!

Ronnie was quite a hit in the play, "Friends & Enemies."

Ronnie bagged the largest Dall Sheep in Alaska.

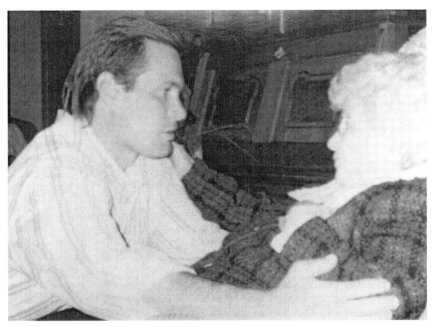

Ronnie loved his grandma! He was the apple of her eye.

My sister, Phyllis, had a tough life. She was my best friend.

Ronnie finally has a brother – 24-years later.

He had a wonderful family and was a great dad.

Gina orchestrated building a huge park in Ronnie's memory.

The whole community came out to build
the park in Dolores, Colorado..

Ronnie, normally camera shy, wanted our picture taken snowmobiling. This was taken four months prior to his passing.

The Fish Is Singing!

About seven months after our devastating loss and well before our first reading with Lee, Gina had some startling things happen that, upon reflection, I am convinced were nudges from Ronnie to let her know he was there. For instance, she and I tried so hard to get tickets to the John Edward's show. He is an acclaimed psychic medium, author and had a daily T.V. show at the time. We tried as I recall on the first Tuesday or Wednesday night of each month at the specific time designated to make phone calls to be on his show. Our hope, of course, was that Ronnie would come through to him if we were in the audience. We would just keep dialing Gina from Colorado and me from Michigan to try to be the fortunate ones to have an operator answer our calls so we could get tickets. This went on for months, all to no avail. All we could get were busy signals. We had read every book he had written to that point. But a strange pattern developed.

I was visiting Gina and the boys during a break in my schedule. John Edward's TV show was broadcast at 4:00 P.M. every weekday. Gina told me not to be surprised if the fish started singing to alert her to turn the TV on to his program. She had a Billy Bass plastic or rubber fish on the fireplace mantle. It was mounted on a board but the tail would flap and it would sing a few bars of "Take me to the river, throw me in the water." Well, it happened to be 4:00 P.M. and we were sitting in the kitchen having a cup of coffee in full view of the fish. We had become lost in our conversation — our "remembering's of Ronnie" and had forgotten to turn on the TV. All of a sudden the fish began to sing. I am not kidding! My mouth dropped open and Gina went over and turned on the TV to the John Edwards' show. She said it happened frequently. I was there for a few days and believe me it happened more than once if we had forgotten to tune in to the program. If the TV was on and we could hear the program the fish remain silent.

Ronnie said at one of my sessions with Lee, *"There is a vulnerability when someone dies; it allows those who love them to grasp onto this magic moment to stay connected. You had to go to that cold, dark place when I left so that you could explain to people that you have been there too."* He added, *"Death is like taking a trip. When people say, 'See you later,' it's true, because you will. It is not the end. It is just like moving to a new location and starting a new beginning. Everyone can experience this type of communication that we have if they want to do it. You are now doing your soul work. You had to live through so much in order to be able to understand and to write this to help others. Happy is the heart that helps. I am so proud of us! You have always been a spokesperson. You just didn't know that you would have a bigger megaphone. Now we can be in collaboration together. We couldn't have done this before when I was on earth because we both would have been too busy. Just remember that sometimes you can't get to people with dynamite. Plant the seed and if they spit it out it's okay. This book is all about being present, being still and letting it come. You have been preparing your whole life for this you just didn't know it. It is fun to talk with you through the writing. You hear me loud and clear."*

This particular message was like a revelation to me. Now I was beginning to understand the 'why' about so many things in my life. It was as if Ronnie switched a light bulb on in my mind. I was able to move out of the darkness. It seemed that all of the losses in my life were meant to serve a higher purpose. It both humbled and amazed me.

When you are able to communicate with your loved one it makes your load easier to carry. Grief, regret and loneliness are like heavy rocks in your backpack. You move in slow motion, think in slow motion and loose your vitality for life. Opening the lines of communication gives you the strength to go on. Your feelings of being hopeless and helpless disappear. You are no longer afraid of the future and realize there is a bigger plan in this Universe and we must all continue to live and learn our own lessons. Ronnie has said so many times, *"Everything is as it should be."* This statement repeated by him has changed my life. I realize now that when difficult life-changing events occur there is a reason, it is not by happenstance. It has given me the ability to relax a bit and accept issues as they crop up. I have given up the thought that I can fix everything. I realize now that some people and some things are in our path for specific reasons. It is not my job to rescue them. In fact, it is a disservice to them to constantly try to fix their unique problems. They have their own lessons to learn, as I do, and I must back off and allow them the challenge of dealing with their life situations without my intervention. As each of us struggle through our latest concerns we are learning our own unique lessons that we have chosen to work on in order to become better people. Before you think this idea or my communication with my family is too strange to believe, please, please withhold judgment and read on. I will share more snippets of the twenty-five documented communications over the past decade that I have had with them. Ronnie has continued to tell me, "We are *just behind the door.*"

Cancer — Messages of Hope and Eventualities

My niece, Suzie, at thirty-six-years old found a tiny lump in one breast on a Friday morning. Concerned, she called her sister and they set up an immediate doctor's appointment. The following Wednesday, she learned she had breast cancer, grade three, stage two and needed immediate medical help. Exactly one week from discovering the lump she was at the Mayo Clinic Hospital in Minneapolis. The timing was perfect. The Universe was working its' magic for her. She was able to meet and work with the head of the Breast Cancer Clinic. A radical mastectomy was performed four days later. After running a series of tests, the doctors discovered that she had all three BRCA (I, II, III) mutations in her genes. These are a genetic coding determined through the lymph nodes that indicate a predisposition for cancer. After a complete mastectomy she then needed sixteen chemo treatments. When she would get sick after the chemo treatments she would look at it as a good thing. The treatment was taking hold! She maintained an uncompromising attitude throughout the treatments that she would beat this cancer and live to raise her three children. She opted for a complete hysterectomy a year later since estrogen seems to be a trigger for this type of cancer. Later we were all excited when she had breast reconstruction and had "boobs" again! She is on medication for seven years with annual evaluations at Mayo. In addition to a full time job, four-year-old twin boys, a nine-year-old son and husband, she donates her time on a weekly basis to fundraisers for the Susan G. Komen organization of Michigan. She is a tremendous example of strength and tenacity.

Upon first hearing about the lump, all of the family members were concerned and frightened. Cancer was not something we had on our side of the family. Hearing the news I called Lee for an appointment. I needed the 'big guns' on this one. Lee worked me in quickly within the next couple of days. This was the first time in any reading that my sister, Suzie's mother began to talk first. She was obviously waiting to talk with me. She shared a great deal about the situation and about the feelings of being vulnerable and afraid. Thinking that your body has betrayed you is especially difficult to accept when you are so physically active and aware of healthy eating habits. Suzie had been a runner and was very athletic, enjoyed pushing her body to develop even greater strength. Phyllis and Ronnie joined forces then and continued to talk about the importance of letting love into your heart. The Black Eyed Peas have a song entitled, "Where Is The Love." It is a rap song that is an incredible social commentary on the world and our place in it. The lyrics, "if you never know truth, you never know love..." were so powerful and appropriate for her situation. They went on to emphasize that loving, laughing and trusting while following a careful medical regimen would be very, very important for her to do. The prognosis from our family on the other side was good — very good — considering the aggressiveness of this type of cancer. They said that initial surgery would be needed as well as more surgery later on but the results would be good. (This was before any surgery had even taken place.) What a relief I felt upon hearing the news! Two years later we can continue to celebrate the remarkable results — thanks to the incredible medical treatment, my niece's attitude of, "*This will not stop me,*" God, of course, and our family on the other side for getting us all together for this one. We have a success story to celebrate.

A few months after Suzie's first surgery, I received another call involving the word cancer.

I had been in Boston conducting a training program for board members of a non-profit organization when I received an email from the daughter of a close friend. It said simply, "Have you talked with my Mom recently?" Standing outside the airport on a gray afternoon waiting to go in to board the plane, I just knew immediately that there was a problem involving health issues. I didn't know who or what was involved but knew I needed to contact her mother, Shelly, immediately. After reaching her, she told me that she had just been diagnosed with stage four, rectal cancer. Naturally she was petrified. She was trying to decide which doctors to use, whether to go to Mayo or stay with local doctors in Michigan and if so, which treatment protocol to agree to. It sounded as if many different options were being presented to her and is was so difficult for her to decide what to do since she was still in a state of shock, as we all would be. Shelly went on to explain that she had fallen getting out of a kayak and thought she had hurt her tailbone. After the pain persisted for a few weeks she went to see a doctor and received the dreadful news. She seemed to be frozen with indecision and was wavering on this monumental decision that could result in her life or death. Meanwhile the cancer kept attacking her body. She then decided on a course of treatment with a doctor in Michigan. We were talking by phone three to four times per week, and I could tell by her voice that she was not getting any better. Sometimes late at night when she was so frightened that she couldn't sleep, she would call and I would listen as she cried and talked about the future. Listening is so underrated in our fast-paced society. I believe the best gift you can give people is to truly listen to them with an empathetic ear. It shows them you care and gives them a lifeline of hope regardless of how thin the line may be.

One month later, during the Thanksgiving weekend my son and I met in Michigan to celebrate Thanksgiving with our extended family and to see Shelly. Together we took her to visit the local cancer clinic and spent some quality time together. I remember looking at her frail body and thinking, "she is not going to make it." She did not have any energy or strength. You could feel the life force being sucked right out of her. She reminded me of the sculpture by Rodin, The Caryatid, which is of a woman collapsing under the burden of her huge "stone." She was indeed collapsing under the weight of her huge stone — cancer.

Flying back to Denver after that weekend I just had a feeling that she would not last long. Over the next few months she and I continued to talk three or four times weekly about her treatment protocol, her hopes and especially her fears.

I had just had knee surgery, sold my house in Golden and was planning a move to Arizona. I went to see Lee to talk to my family on the other side about the situation. I wondered if I should fly back to Michigan and stay for a few weeks to try to help Shelly out emotionally and relieve the family, given her treatment schedule. I knew the ice and snow in Michigan would be tricky to maneuver with my recent surgery but was willing to do anything I could to help out.

Ronnie immediately came into the reading and said, *"Don't even think of getting on a plane now. You have to heal from your knee surgery and it will take a lot of energy to move to Arizona. You will have time to help her later."* He said that *"after a few phone calls down the road they will tell you that there is nothing more they can do and she will need you then."*

Three months and many, many phone calls later, the call that Ronnie had told me about came in March 2010. Immediately after meeting with the doctors, her daughter and then Shelly called. The news was devastating. The doctors had told her they were going to stop the treatments and that there was nothing more they could do. They would try to keep her as comfortable as possible. The cancer had spread to her lung area and there were even more spots on her liver. The treatments had not stopped the aggressiveness of the cancer. It had been diagnosed too late. Shelly added with a small, grief stricken voice the rest of the news relayed by the doctors — she had only a few months, maybe up to six, left to live. She added in a scarcely audible voice, *"Will you be here with me when it is time?"* Neither one of us could use the word death. I responded, *"Of course I will,"* as I tried to hide the fear and sadness in my voice. She was just fifty-eight years old. How could this be happening to her?

She was still talking about whether to try to get to Mayo to see if something else could be done. As the days on the calendar ticked off and we continued to talk frequently by phone, I still couldn't get a definitive time when to fly to Michigan. I explained I could make more than one trip. I kept waiting but still no answer came as to the best time to come and help. Finally, one day I was sitting at my computer and I just "heard" the dates when I needed to travel. I immediately made reservations to fly to Michigan from April 15th to the 29th. After doing so, I called her family and said I would be there in two weeks. I had been taking the training for Hospice volunteers, in the meantime, and was nearly finished by the time I was to leave for Michigan. It was an immense help and allowed me to be better prepared to help her and know what to ask for if specific items had not been previously supplied. We were able to get oxygen tanks, a walker and various changes to her medication. She had been crawling on hands and knees, at times, to the bathroom and was relieved to realize that by using a walker she actually felt better and was in less pain since she was able to stretch out her spine. She began sleeping on the couch in the living room, unable to make it upstairs to the bedroom. She liked me to sleep in the recliner next to the couch since she woke up throughout the night in fear and needed to talk it out. As a result, I was able to be with my friend twenty-four/seven for basically the last two weeks of her life. It was so hard to see her literally waste away. The first week I was with her she wanted to go out to lunch, even though she ate very little — maybe three bites of anything she ordered. She even wanted to go shopping and bought some clothes for the summer. As I was pushing her in her wheel chair around the clothing store I felt so sad for her. She had gone from a size twelve to a size two in a matter or months. Would she really be alive long enough to enjoy these clothes? I decided it really didn't matter. If it gave her joy or just an escape even for a few hours it was worth it. At one point she asked me if I thought it was stupid for her to be buying summer clothes. I responded with feigned confidence, of course not! I had learned in Hospice that everyone's journey is unique unto themselves and you simply follow their lead. The second week, after she insisted that we make a visit to the funeral home to change and ultimately confirm the final arrangements she had made a couple months before, she just seemed to give up. She stopped talking about getting better and seemed resigned herself to the inevitable. Day by day she was getting significantly worse. She was lost in her own thoughts — her own life review during the last five days of our time together. The pain was intolerable and you just wanted to cry for her. I left on the 29th of April to fly back to Phoenix and told her I would be back. On Saturday, two days later, her daughter called me several times expressing her concern and dismay regarding the tremendous pain that her mother was exhibiting. She died later that night in her home with her entire family around her, as it should be.

Shelly was a special person in so many ways. The memories of the fun we had and her giving heart will remain alive forever. A few years earlier, both of our families went on a ski trip to Steamboat Springs. We had the best time and laughed the entire week we were together. I thank her for those times and know that she is now free of the unbearable pain that she had endured. I know she is watching over her grown children and the grandchildren — who she absolutely adored — with the unconditional love that she had for them. I was glad to be able to be there for her when she needed me. The family needed a short break to rest up and gain the strength they would need for this last lap to say good-bye.

Once again, my family on the other side gave me the information to wait, the direction when to make the plane reservations and the love and support when I needed it most. I flew back to Michigan on Tuesday for her upcoming funeral.

I learned through my Hospice training that some of the Hospice organizations are "for profit" and some are "not for profit." You can easily check out the difference by going to the web sites for Hospice in your state. If a particular Hospice organization is not-for-profit it will be clearly designated after their name on the site. If you don't see the designation it is a for profit Hospice organization. I have not met anyone who knew there was a difference. I didn't know before my training. I volunteer for Hospice of the Valley, which is a not-for-profit-organization. It is an important thing to check out when a family member or friend needs to be supported through the end-of-life experience. The Hospice philosophy is to bring dignity and caring to the patient and family during the end-of-life experience and create happy memories for the family. Hopefully, the patient can pass on in their own home surrounded by the sights, sounds and smells that are familiar to them. The Hospice team consisting of doctors, nurses, certified nursing assistants, social workers, chaplains and bereavement counselors. All of these people make volunteers like me feel like an invaluable member of the team.

I read a piece in the newspaper recently that listed the source as anonymous. Whoever wrote it, thank you. It just seemed to make so much sense as we think about our loved ones who are gone from our sight. It reminded me of the many messages I have received from my family on the other side.

"You can shed tears that she is gone or you can smile because she lived.

You can close your eyes and pray that she will be back, or you can open your eyes and see all that she left for you.

Your heart can be empty because you can't see her or it can be full of the love you shared.

You can turn your back on tomorrow and live in the yesterdays or you can be happy for tomorrow because of yesterday.

You can remember only that she is gone or you can cherish the memories and let her live on in your heart.

You can cry and close your mind, be empty and turn your back, or you can do what she would want you to do, smile, open your eyes, *love and remember the great times you had with her and go on."*

I would add a few words to this wonderful tribute,

"You can grieve that she is gone or you can learn how to hear her because she is just behind the door."

Relationships — When the Lessons Are Learned

On the topic of marriage let me just say that although I do not have Elizabeth Taylor's record beat I have had more than my share. Being raised in the 1950s I just thought if you slept with them you married them. Sounds sort of strange saying that in today's culture. I did not live with someone and avoid marriage. For many, short-term affairs are looked upon as no big deal. Sometimes in my more crude moments I would say in answer to the question of my marriages, "I probably have had fewer marriages than you have had sexual affairs. I just chose to make it legal." Not entirely a gracious thing to say but to some people it was true, nonetheless. I have learned many important lessons from these relationships. A huge lesson for me in relationships has been the same one I have dealt with in the rest of my life. I have had to learn to stop enabling people by rushing in to rescue them anytime they sounded in need. I am especially vulnerable to others who use pregnant pauses to initiate a response from me. I am a fixer by nature and I like to help people. I now realize that, as in the rest of life, if you consistently take on other people's issues it often robs them of the important lessons they have chosen to learn in their own life script. However, in the past I had perfected this approach to an art form. My ear is now attuned to listening more carefully for the pregnant pauses and then offering encouragement and confidence that they will resolve their issue. In other words, I have learned when to butt out! Also, being able to say 'No' when I really felt in my gut that I wanted to has been another lesson that has required a great deal of courage and effort to overcome. I no longer worry about hurting someone's feelings when, nicely but firmly, I disagree with them or choose not to go along with their plan. A third lesson is that there are simply no versions of the truth. Truth is truth. When someone gives me only part of an explanation, before responding, I now realize that I have an obligation to seek more information to avoid jumping to erroneous conclusions. Adding these lessons together has resulted in too many "I dos" and not enough "I don'ts." I am getting much better but must admit that I have been a remedial learner!

A dear friend in North Carolina told me that my 'chooser was broken.' She admitted that she also had a 'broken chooser' and that is how she recognized it in me. I thought more about this idea of choosing and realized she was right. I think when God or the Universe was giving out character traits I was in the wrong line for some of them. I missed the one that said, love thyself. Living through the deaths and divorces in my marriages has made me stronger and wiser.

I remember reading a novel in my late twenties about a woman who made a list of all the attributes she wanted in a prospective husband. Can you believe how unromantic and calculating that sounds? Well, depending upon your age and success rate at the institution of marriage you might be saying, as I have come to believe, no — it is not cold nor calculating — but extremely important. Values, goals, belief systems, work ethic, honesty, faithfulness, and educational level are all extremely important in determining compatibility for the long haul. I may sound wise but trust me these were lessons that I did not learn quickly nor easily. It cost me dearly on so many levels to be able to say, I finally get it!

My first two husbands were as different as night and day. Both had different qualities. But they did have one thing in common, the grass — or skirt — always looked better on the other side of the fence. At first you say to yourself, what can I do better or differently and then you realize that some men just want more variety in their lives while the home fires are kept burning. Some research actually suggests that there is a medical condition related to this condition but sadly, no actual medication exists to administer to them and fix the problem. Besides, I wonder exactly where on their body would the medication need to be applied? Exit stage left for me! As challenging as my parents' marriage was, the one thing they did have was complete trust in each other even when they were out of sight.

My next husband died, after only six months of marriage, through suicide. He made sure that his previous attempts at suicide, before meeting me, had been kept hidden during our short dating period. Had I known, I might have been able to help him or at least decide against the union. Although, knowing where I was at the time, I most likely would have given it the good old college try and tried to "fix" him. At his funeral I had the song, "Bridge Over Troubled Waters" sung by a trio. It seemed so fitting. How sad it must be to be so internally troubled that life does not seem worth living, or to hurt so much inside that you cannot feel the love around you. I understand that chronic depression is usually the result of a chemical imbalance. It is critical that people seek out treatment — even life-long medication — if that is what it takes to feel better. The books on loss that I have read have stated that suicide is one of the hardest things for a parent to accept. I imagine it would be and my heart goes out to these parents. When it is your spouse you wonder, were there any tell-tale signs that I missed that could have prevented it from happening? Trying to help someone see that life is worth living and that they are not hopeless or helpless is an extremely exhausting but important thing to do. Ultimately only they can decide to do something about their lives. Knowing that we have individually chosen this life script makes the issue of blame null and void.

My fourth husband died during open-heart surgery. It was his second bypass surgery and although he was such a wonderful human being he was just unable to beat the odds of the heart problems the males in his family had inherited. We did have five wonderful years together. He treated me with such graciousness and embodied the three most important things for a marriage to work — he provided, protected and professed his altruist love for me. I learned from this experience that when you have that kind of mature relationship it is a rare gift.

The day of his surgery the doctors thought it would take about three or four hours and it ended up to be over nine hours. It was just too long for his heart to endure. I remember watching the eyes of the nurse who kept coming out every forty-five minutes or so to give me an update, the severity of the surgery was obviously taking a toll on the surgical team. My parents and best friend, MaryAnn, were with me in the waiting room. At 5:20 P.M. I lifted my cup to take a sip of coffee and literally couldn't breath — I felt that there was no way I could get any air into my lungs. I jumped up and ran out into corridor with my friend running behind. She said, *"What's the matter, doll?"* I looked at her when I could get my breath and asked her the time. She answered that it was 5:20 P.M. I said, *"He just died."* She assured me that he would be okay but I knew better. Sadly, within about ten minutes I was meeting with the doctor who said that he had done everything he could do but that there was too much scar tissue which made the bypass surgery and the new tissue attachment impossibly difficult and too long for his heart. I asked the doctor what time he died — the answer — 5:20 P.M.

My husband and I had discussed the issue just 12 hours before as we were waiting for him to be taken down to surgery. I told him that if he saw the other side and decided to leave, I would be okay. I did ask him to promise me one thing — to let me know first, before being told by the doctor. He assured me that he would. Always true to his word, he gave me the message when he died, the air just left my lungs. Everything in the Universe, cells, molecules and atoms are made up of energy. As human beings we are energy at our core. It is no wonder he was able to tap into the energy of unconditional love to communicate to me his decision to cross over.

About two years later I tried the marriage thing "one more time for old time's sake." Knowing that my track record was not particularly good I was beyond hesitant to say the least. At this point in my life, the lesson, of saying no when I really wanted to, was still unlearned. After time and serious soul searching, my initial hesitancy gave way and we were married. I believe I gave it all I had to give. Nearly one and a half years later I was blessed at 42 years old to have a second son. He is not only the light of my life but likely the reason this union needed to take place. He was the individual that I needed in my life to get me through the loss of Ronnie. His father and I were given the ultimate gift, an amazing child that was an old, wise soul from the moment he took his first breath. A powerful surfactant in our relationship, he was the attractor that kept two immiscible elements (one that conducted electricity and the other that dampened it) together for all of those years. Unfortunately, the Universe had other plans or had decided I still had not learned my lesson. After dating for two years, this marriage lasted twenty-three. I was then faced with what had become a life theme for me: loss and moving on — with regret and sadness.

It seemed impossible to believe that this was happening again. I discovered that when two people sap each other's life force, a fix is not to be found. It was time to bite the bullet and move on! There are no rights or wrongs, just differences — extreme differences — in this case. When you are no longer working sixty to sixty-five hours per week and actually have the time in life to observe your situation it can be sobering, to say the least. What started out as a potentially good situation — slowly disintegrated into a burden too heavy to carry — remember Rodin's sculpture entitled "Caryatid." As we grew older, the differences in our perspectives on life were glaringly obvious. Waking one morning I had an epiphany! In some ways I was becoming my mother and my husband was becoming my father. Whoa! Their union may have lasted sixty-four years but how sad it was to watch them as they sapped the energy from each other, found less and less to celebrate and eventually nothing to cherish

Looking back now, I am not sure we really have a choice about who we fall in love with at a particular time in our lives. But we do have a choice about who we marry. It is only fair to both parties to painstakingly consider a list of similarities and differences before entering into a union. Each person needs to be true to their unique self in a marriage for it to survive. When the differences are examined they still can be accommodated if, and this is a big if, your love and concern for them is truly altruistic. It takes the mind of a pragmatist and the heart of a romantic in combination to make such an important and critical decision.

Once I had decided to move on I had a reading with Lee. My mother came through immediately. *"You had the courage to do what I should have done. It is time to move on. Don't think of it as a failure but just remember the lessons learned."* The great news was, in addition to so many lessons learned from this relationship, we had produced one dynamite son, so we both have a little piece of immortality for which to be thankful.

During this reading, Ronnie added, *"Some times people are just not the right fit for each other. They are on different wavelengths, different vibrations maybe even from different planets! And when the lessons that needed to be learned from each other are learned, it may be time for both people to move on. It does not mean it was a failure, it was simply a lesson learned to completion."* Completion, now that was a thought I had to process through the recesses of my mind more fully. When I explained to Lee that the divorce was finalized at 9:00 A.M. on the ninth day of the ninth month in 2009. She knowingly responded, "Nine is a sign of completion in numerology." The Universe, once again, wanted to get my attention!

My sister chimed in, *"The time was perfect and now the time has passed. The cake is baked. Take it out of the oven before it burns. You have never had balance in your life. You have always been taking care of everyone else even as a little girl. You don't need this project anymore. The goose is cooked! Now don't feel like you have to juggle anyone's balls in the air."* Her on target one liners never ceased to shock and amaze me when she was alive. Interestingly, she continues to demonstrate this character trait even from the other side. It often results in a peal of laughter because she is so spot on about things, rather like a laser light that illuminates only the miniscule essential of the issue. She added, *"Each person is on their own path. You don't have to be the ring leader anymore."* She ended by saying, *"I love you. You don't have a selfish bone in your body. What you do have now is more self-awareness. It is about balance, what you want and need in your life. What you need is serenity and joy and you are working on both of those things. The dark cloud has passed. It is important to feel all of your feelings without judging if they are good or bad. Even depression is important. You learned to have more compassion and tolerance for people who are depressed."*

Ronnie added, *"You have always just pushed harder to make things happen. Don't be discouraged. You really did bring justice where there wasn't any. People had no idea about your intensity! You had to speak up for yourself. Mom, you no longer have to continue to live your life like it is a project and take care of someone else. Now you can stop and have some fun."* He continued, *"Certain people knew how to play on your Catholic guilt"* that had been internalized throughout my early upbringing. *"They knew how to make you feel sorry for them."* All that was becoming so clearer to me now. I must have had some karma to work through and had to be one of the slowest learners ever created! He went on, *" You needed to go through all this stuff for self-revelation. This loss brought up the grieving about me that you put a rug over the last time while you just kept working to support the family. It has all come up to you at once. You were able to do this difficult and fantastic work with yourself for your own growth."*

I was somewhat relieved upon hearing the explanation but when he used the word "fantastic," I must admit that it didn't feel fantastic. I knew this change had to happen in my life. So why couldn't I shake the feelings of depression that I was having? Although, I had lived through a great deal of challenges and tragedies in my life, I had always thought to myself, just put one foot in front of the other and go on. It is a mantra that both my boys live by as well. This time that type of self-talk just wasn't working. It was humbling and a little frightening to say the least that I couldn't just snap out of it.

Thank God and the Universe for my family and friends. They kept in close contact and, without mentioning it at the time, were walking this journey with me ready at a moment's notice to jump in further and help in any way. Strangely, friends from twenty-five years ago seemed to magically reappear back into my life. Ronnie added, *"I'm sorry you have had to go through these challenging times but you are letting others give to you. That has not been your strong suit. To allow yourself to feel vulnerable has been so difficult but this has been a good lesson for you."* When you experience this type of selfless caring and concern from family and friends — near and far — you realize the power and importance of unconditional love.

Mom continued, *"We know you hear us all the time. We are happy that we can all connect.* Ronnie added, *"We are right in your heartbeat Mom. You hear me laughing! You are getting it. You have to let it come to you. Patience is not a strong suit for you either."* When he was on this physical plane he had about enough patience to fill a small — very small — thimble. The good news is that the love from my family and friends continues on. Unconditional loss can't be dismissed but the energy involved in unconditional love is the life blood of our existence.

Ronnie went on to explain that it is about trusting. *"Everyone has their own soul path and everything is as it should be. You can only affect your own circle. You have to let others figure out their own burdens and shoulder them. You now realize that you are vulnerable and you are here to learn that loving yourself is important. It is not just about loving others. Always giving to others is like feeding your ego. To receive is to balance your soul life. You are beginning to actually practice it. It is better to give than receive BUT you give to others when you receive from them as well. It is keeping the world in balance. You have to receive as much as you give."*

Well, I decided that I had blown it after hearing that last part! Being raised in a tradition that taught me to be humble and give to others, I had, once again, taken it to the extreme. I had forgotten about myself along the way. I truly thought I was giving to others to make them happy or their lives easier, not to feed my ego. Apparently not! I certainly had a lot to learn in yet another area. Learning to receive was a big lesson, indeed. It is something I am still working on to this day.

I needed to live through these experiences in life to internalize the many lessons presented in them. I know now that if we experience a significant loss of any type in our lives and, as my British grandmother used to say, *"Just keep a stiff upper lip,"* sometimes that works, but most often it really doesn't — at least — not in the long haul. Our emotions don't just evaporate into thin air. Likewise, if we ignore our feelings just to keep peace in a relationship, sooner or later those feelings will rise to the surface with an intensity that lays bare the depth of resentment that has been growing over the years. The longer we keep burying our feelings, our truth about who we are, the deeper and more intensely we have to dig to unearth them. In Arizona, they would call that type of digging a hard dig and you pay dearly for it.

Real Estate and Reassurances

In addition to the messages of life, death, endings and celebrations that I have received from my family behind the door, other life changing events have also been communicated to me. Words of hope, encouragement and faith in the future were always uplifting to hear. I use to perseverate on so many issues concerning buying and selling property. I could get myself so worked up thinking about the 'what ifs' that I could even make myself nervous! I am not kidding here. Luckily, I have been taught by my family on the other side to slow down and let life unfold. There is an incredible peace in doing so.

With real estate, I am cautious, make a mental list of the do's and don'ts about buying a particular piece of property and plan in advance for the eventual time for resale. Actually, I am quite methodological about the whole thing. My heart does not rule my head on property and I am not afraid to say "No" to an offer. No wonder I have had better luck with real estate than husbands!

When I was nine months away from retirement I knew the house needed to be on the market but I was worried that if it sold immediately where would we live for a short period? We had a 5,200 square-foot white stucco ranch on ten acres. It was beautiful inside and out. It was also filled to the brim with stuff. Would all of the stuff we had accumulated in twenty-three years need to be put in storage? What would be the added costs for two moves rather than one — my worries just went on and on. My family joked at times and said that I had a "Degree in Worry." Sad but true.

I used to think to myself when I heard that rather glib comment directed to me, well, someone better worry, the house payment needs to be made and food bought for the table. It was enlightening to me when years later I learned that the more I worried the less those close to me did — on purpose! Why didn't I see the pattern? Although I know of people who just slide through life and wait for things to happen I was never one of them. These people seem to get rescued by others at every twist and turn in their life. Do they send out an intention of being taken care of or being rescued purposely? It amazes me to this day. Ultimately, very few people get a free ride in life unless they have some unusual tools. I was more the type that didn't mind hard work and wanted to make things happen. I now believe the best approach is the melding of both perspectives. Using the gift of free will to set the intentions in motion by planning and actively working toward a goal but then be at peace in the faith that the Universe will provide for you in the right time and place.

My sister came to me in a reading and said, *"Honey, you have a beautiful home and it may feel like you need a crowbar to leave it but there will be an opportunity to leave Michigan and it will be fantastic."* She added, *"You will move out of state, to a temporary place first and then to something more permanent."* She continued, *"I see boxes everywhere."* Mom chimed in with a critical piece of information, *"Three different families will be interested in the house on the same weekend."* Ronnie elaborated, *"A family that has been in the house before would buy it and everything will work out. Get to packing!"*

It happened just as they told me it would. Three different families were interested in the same timeframe. A wonderful couple that were business colleagues of mine and had been in the house many times, bought the house in September and allowed us to rent it back from them until my retirement in July! I never knew they were even faintly interested in it until I received a call from them. What would the chances be of selling your house and being allowed to rent it back for nine months? The Universe truly does provide and in perfect timing!

After my retirement we moved back to Denver and lived in a 1,000-square-foot apartment for five months before buying a home in the town of Golden just fifteen minutes from the city. After some minor remodeling and decorating the house, there was little left to do but watch the slow disintegration of our marriage. My husband had moved out and I was trying to sell the house and make preparations to move to Phoenix. During this seven-month period, everything seemed to need replacement or repair. I just couldn't get a break. The furnace, air conditioner, roof, appliances, some carpet and even both fireplaces developed gas leaks in them simultaneously! The list went on and on. It felt like I was throwing money down a black hole but had no choice to stop. At one point when I was sprucing up the bathrooms just twenty minutes before a house showing, and thinking how much worse can it get when the sink in the guest bathroom literally came off from the wall. Seriously? This house seemed like a real albatross. I often wondered while struggling to make it all work financially, will this ever end? Money was going out a lot quicker than it was coming in since I was in retirement and picking up just a few jobs as a consultant from time to time. To escape the insidious situation even for an hour I had set up a meeting with Lee. At this reading Ronnie said, "*Stop worrying, the house will sell and the closing will go off without a hitch.*" My mom and sister added that all three of them would be at the closing with me and, "*I would know it when something with the papers and water happened.*" I was so relieved to know the house would sell, given the down market in 2009 and coupled with the need to complete a property settlement for the divorce, that I completely forgot about the water and paper signal. I felt hopeful, after visiting Lee once again and hearing from my loved ones that everything would work out. Immediately, I regrouped and began more positive self talk while I put all my energy into making sure the house was in excellent shape for every showing. I was just waiting for the one buyer I needed to come through and say they would take it.

The offer came through on the house the same day I blew out my knee and found out that I would need surgery. My knee looked and felt about three times its' normal size. My doctor told me — when exercising, moderation is a better approach at my age. I was quite shocked! Seriously, I just had not accepted the fact that getting older meant doing things a bit differently. Why not go for the gold and push yourself? Well, with that attitude I ended up using a crutch for three weeks before surgery to relieve the intense pain from any movement. I received a call the night I blew out my knee. The prospective buyers wanted to go through the house again the following morning. I grabbed my crutch and the vacuum and started to sweep the carpet. All three levels needed to be in tip top shape. After completing this task I realized that I needed to go out and shovel the snow off from the walk and driveway. I put on my ski outfit to protect me from the frigid cold and hobbled out on the crutch. There was black ice under the snow on the sloping driveway and after shoveling the snow off and throwing salt on it to melt I'd had it! I had fallen two times in the process and was feeling pretty sorry for myself. I thought — OK guys, you said this would be fine, it sure isn't feeling that way! However, after the buyers went through the house a second time, an offer and counter offer were made and accepted and a contract to sell was presented to me the next day. The date for the house closing was set for January 28, 2010.

I was desperate and needed someone who would roll up their sleeves and finish the packing, help me hire movers to put my things in storage and help me through surgery. I called Lois, my best friend in Arizona, and humbled myself and asked for her help, big time. This was a lesson I was working on — to take as well as give. Without a second thought she jumped in her car and headed for Denver. She came and stayed for a month to finish the packing and help me through surgery. I wanted a particular surgeon who had been highly recommended at the sports rehab clinic I was sent to after the CAT scan. Consequently I had to wait until January 8th to have it done. Surgery was successful even though at times I felt an amputation would have been less painful.

The movers came and the house was totally vacant and cleaned on the day of the closing. Everything had gone off without a hitch thanks to a little — no, actually a lot — of help from my friend. As you may have guessed by now, near the end of signing the papers, I accidently spilled water from my glass on the corner of the papers! I did not even feel my hand touch the glass. I had bought and sold 12 different houses in my life and never once spilled anything on the paperwork. The water didn't do any real harm and was easily absorbed with paper towels but got my attention and caused me to flash back and remember what my family had told me. They would be with me at the closing and I would know it with an issue involving paper and water. Thanks guys for giving me a visible sign that you are always with me.

My doctor reviewed his surgical work and said I could drive the 14 hours to Phoenix but would need to get out every two hours to walk and exercise. Lois and I left for Arizona about fifteen minutes after the closing. It was snowing in Denver, which is not unusual in late January, and I just kept thinking, it will get better as we drive south. By the time we had reached southern Colorado it was a white out and the highway was literally a path with one set of tire tracks in it. If you are a downhill skier these conditions can be tricky but fun. In a caravan of two cars, both filled to overflowing with stuff that I might need in Phoenix until I found a house to move into and adding Lois's dog to the scene, we looked like gypsies driving across country. It was treacherous nighttime driving and even with the low beam headlights, the blowing snow was blinding. We decided we better not go any further and stopped to get gas and find lodging for the night. No luck on the lodging. Every thing was booked for the next seventy-five miles the convenience store employee told us. He said he had just called around for another group of people and knew nothing was available. At times we were driving fifteen miles per hour. By the time we reached Flagstaff, Arizona, the next day, they were digging out of a record ten feet of snow that had been dumped on them. I thought, with trepidation, I hope this isn't a sign of things to come. But then I mentally reviewed my last seven months. I had lived through one catastrophe after another with the house, extensive knee surgery, and the completion of a divorce settlement. I had just lived through a real pile of dodo and a pony had to be in there somewhere! I kept remembering what Ronnie had told me many times since his death, "All is as it should be.' I inhaled and exhaled slowly and remembered to have faith in the future.

At a previous reading, Ronnie talked about my new life that was unfolding. *"You will be very happy in Arizona, develop new friendships and have your pick of houses."* He added, *"I am so happy for you because you are freeing yourself up. It is a wonderful feeling that you can take a breath and not always be thinking about someone else. You have just crossed the finish line of this marathon."*

Then he offered a suggestion, *"Mom, I know you don't want to hear this but you need to rent first to be sure you select the right area, being right in the city would not be something you would be happy with."* Renting was not in my mental plan. I have always liked the stability and responsibility of owning my own home and seem to have that nesting instinct. Lois let me stay with her while I was searching for a place to buy. Finally after looking at forty-five homes in one week, which gave my knee a real workout, I told her I had narrowed it down to two homes, and asked her to give me her opinion. She looked at both of them and was not excited about either one. She asked me if I really loved them. The look on my face made the answer quite obvious. She suggested that I continue looking and mentioned a part of the valley that I had not even considered.

I found the location in the northwest valley of Phoenix and the model home that I loved two days later. Best of all, I could actually afford it given the nosedive that the housing market had taken in Arizona. But waiting five months? How could I do that, where would I live? Lois, once again, came through for me. She said in a matter-of-fact way " *Just stay here with me.*" She reluctantly let me pay rent while I lived with her. Ronnie told me to rent but I would never have considered this renting. My vision of renting was an apartment — the typical thing you think about when the term renting comes up. When I mentioned to her that Ronnie had said to rent and I wasn't doing that, she corrected me — I was renting just not in the way I had envisioned! I will be forever grateful for her tremendous help and willingness to open her home to me for such a long period of time. When you have a friend that genuinely cares about you and asks nothing in return it is a gift from heaven! I learned another important lesson: when the other side communicates to us, if we put our preconceived notions aside, we will hear and understand more clearly.

After purchasing the lot and selecting the model I thought was just perfect, I pulled out my notes from Ronnie, and again was totally surprised. Reviewing what I had purchased, I could put a check mark next to everything he pointed out. He had said, *"The area that you move to will be beautifully landscaped, the construction very solid. The area has been settled for a few years. You will be out of the city a few miles. It will have nice parks around it and life is going on, it feels alive."* He went on to say, *"The area, would have space around me."* I have a hill (they call it a mountain here) in my backyard. This home is my sanctuary. Everything about it is peaceful, joyful and the surrounding parks and over 3 miles of walking trails allow me to take my dog, Buddy, a sixty-pound Australian Shepherd on walks. He is incredibly protective, shows his love in so many ways, and provides me the distractions I need to stay balanced. I agree with Shirley MacLaine's statement in her recent book, I'm Over All That, when she talks about her preference to have a dog rather than a man in her life. Buddy is much easier to satisfy, thrilled when he gets a treat or a pat on the head and just wants to give and receive love — no strings attached.

A brick wall in our path may not be intended to prevent us from achieving something but to teach us a lesson. I know with the deaths of my son, mother, sister and husbands and the challenges of my marriages, the individual bricks that made up my wall consisted of acceptance, learning I could not control everything, asking for help from others and staying true to myself by saying, 'No,' when I intuitively felt the need to do so. I had always felt that if I just tried harder, worked harder I could make everything work for everyone. With these life changing events, I realized there are some things that are not simply, 'mind over matter.' I couldn't go around, through, over or under these bricks. I needed to face them straight on and learn the lessons they presented. It was as if the bricks had neon lights in them and were flashing at me to understand and accept the messages. Although I couldn't change things or bring my beloved family back in a physical sense, I realized my avocation since the early 1970s had been an intentional preparation for my next stage in life. I just try to remember each day what Ronnie has said to me, *"It's all as it should be."*

I know, in every part of my being, that there are no 'endings' — just new beginnings. The unconditional love that I have for my family, here and on the other side, has enabled me to find more patience with today and trust in tomorrow. I no longer live in the sadness of the past — in the "what was" ... but instead choose to live in the mindset of what "still is".... . There truly is a reason for everything that happens, even when it may take fifty years to understand and see the bigger picture. What a humbling and reassuring thing to know that our loved ones behind the door are ready, so very willing, and able to offer guidance and help to us. We are never truly alone.

Communicate with Your Loved Ones Behind the Door

In January I met with Lee and immediately, Ronnie came through and talked again about the first of three books I was to write. He said, *"See Mom, there is something good in everything that happens. You must write the first part of this book about my death. You know how it was for you. You need to say your piece first and then I will add my part. Just remember that love may be an intangible but it can be felt. I know that you can hear me. Remember that accepting what IS eliminates the pain. The mask of death is the vacant part of the soul that has left the earth. People love so much that they want their loved ones to live forever but the door must be revolving."*

He continued, *"Everyone needs to know that nothing really dies."* The essence of the person, the soul, the spirit is always with us through our unconditional love connection. The core message is that everyone can experience this connection. We are all just behind the door ready to connect with our loved ones once again."

My mom and sister advised me to, *"Allow some spaces in your life. Don't hurry up to fill them in. This is the first time in many years that you have been in this space. You need time for solitude and making connections with the Universe. Now is the time to dive in deeply to your essence. Take time for quiet reflection."*

Ronnie jokingly added, *"You are creating a book of, 'Rememberances' and I'm the special feature!"* He went on to say, *"Love is eternal and it is the way to stay connected."* He said I would, *"Be teaching and speaking but not on the subjects that you think you would be working on"* (my field is education and organizational leadership). *"You will be talking about the essence — the esoteric — and all will flow. Love is the way to stay connected. You will really be helping people put their feelings back together. Some people like to stay stuck because it stops them from opening the door. It is the nature of humans to be here in the senses that they are familiar with. When you are in a body everything seems so real. But love is both a physical sense and it is also an unseen sense."*

I was both surprised and a bit intimidated to think that I would be writing a book for public consumption. Did I really want to share all of this? Some of it is, indeed, a bit dicey. I had been successful in my educational career but this was something else altogether. As I thought about it for sometime, I realized that if it could help others who have lost a loved one and are stuck in grief or anger it would be worth it. To help others realize their loved one is waiting to reconnect with them could change their lives forever. If it took me sharing my baggage to help others, so be it. I had planned on writing a biography of Ronnie for his children. I wanted them to know what a great dad they had and still have to this day. They were so young when he died that they really didn't know him. That book is yet to be written. It will be when the time is right. I was told by my family on the other side to write this one first and follow with two others. It all became clearer to me as I thought about the timing. The many "opportunities" that Ronnie was involved in during his life would be better read by his twins after they graduated from high school and not quite this soon. Sometimes it is better not to give young boys ideas about how to test the system!

Ronnie continued to encourage me to start writing by saying, *"The book you will be writing is not about religion but about love and spirit. Death is natural and it happens to all."* For emphasis he then repeated from a reading one year before, *"How wonderful that you love someone so much that* you want to have them live forever. But the door always needs to be revolving. It's the law of the Universe. To accept what is, helps to eliminate pain. Death is intangible just like love is intangible but it can be felt. These conversations that we have are beyond uplifting, more than just making you happy. It's like, let's have a cup of coffee but you don't need to pour mine! Relax into the knowing that there are many, many worlds and they are all connecting. You always had this belief but you had to experience it to make it real. The intangible has now become real."*

He then cautioned, *"Mom, you are like a great fisherman. Some people won't want to be caught in the net but it's okay. For some, staying in the grief is looked upon as staying connected. Some people might think if they really accept the sadness and really take it in, they may end up to be nothing more than a puddle on the floor and not ever able to get it together again. I know that one of my sons feel reluctant to let go of the memory of the accident. He is afraid that if he lets go of the trauma of the accident then he would let go of me. He has been punishing himself all of this time thinking there was something he could have done to prevent the accident. He could not have done anything to prevent it. It was meant to be. Some people feel that it is wrong to be happy. It is not wrong to be happy. Remember the good times, the fun times and talk about us. We are with you always!"*

Ronnie gave me further encouragement. *"Try to get people turned on to themselves. The key is inside of them. When you talked about wishing that you could see me one last time, I thought about all of you like that too. I think of it as a photo album and I look at the pictures but not the part that isn't filled in on the pages of the album. We will fill those pages in later. Everyone needs to know that nothing dies. The spirit, the soul, lives on. Love and communication continues forever if people will open themselves up to it."*

He assured me that he was doing great. *"I'm learning a lot. I'm fine, couldn't be better. I learn so much here and go to something that looks like a huge library with a dome. There is never a dull moment. It's like I think of someone and they are here on this side and I see them. Just like we do with each other. There is really no time or space, it is like infinity."*

He went on, *"Mom, don't worry. You are walking a golden path that many have walked before you. They have been spreading rose petals along the path and now you are spreading your own wisdom. It's like a fire extinguisher. You have to break the glass to help others address their emergency with grief. They need to have an emergence to see. Don't worry about convincing all — some people will insist on keeping the shutters down. They hold on to their tears not realizing that many of us can feel and see the grief in their eyes."*

Actual tears of sadness and grief in people are evident. One only needs to see them in another person to realize they need a comforting word, a hug or maybe a shoulder to lean on. Listening with empathy as they repeat the stories of their loss is an important thing to do for them. Each time they verbalize their grief it is an opportunity for healing. They are trying to work through their loss but are a bit unsteady in the new and uncertain world they find themselves in. Their existence seems to be measured by a 'before death' or 'after death' designation in their environment. Other people experience this uncertainty but demonstrate a tearless grief, which is even more insidious. Their tears appear hidden from initial view but the devastating toll their grief is taking on every cell of their body demonstrate its' power. You look into their eyes and see a sadness so deep, that it causes you to stop and wonder, what on earth has happened to them. They may be immobilized by fear of the unknown, of the tomorrows, unable to move beyond the initial stages in the grief process. These people also need to be listened to but in a way so profound that they can feel the caring, concern and belief you have in their ability to heal and move forward in life. They need to know they can rely on you to be there for them for as long as it takes. It's as if your world stops spinning while you zero in on their grief and share your confidence that they will emerge from their feelings of utter despair. Slowly, they will rebuild a belief in a more positive tomorrow as you gently hold their arms as a guide on the side through their devastating journey of loss. This is essential since their experience of the yesterdays have taken their trust in the tomorrows away. They gain emotional strength and energy from your presence and will be able to push through their barrier of grief. As we gently and lovingly question them about their loss, the floodgates holding back their wall of tears will release and allow the depth of their grief to surface. They may not even realize that they have become the walking wounded and it has profoundly changed them. When you take the time to listen with both your heart and your mind you give them a chance to process their sadness and release the pent up tears that have made them a shell of the person they once were. Slowly, they will regain their foothold in today and belief in tomorrow. The healing energy between two people is the salve that is needed on the wounds. Just as prayer is healing the loving presence and selfless caring for others is also healing. It is that simple and that profound.

My mom and sister gave me their loving touch and selfless caring when I was at the lowest point in my life. They listened without judgment and cared beyond measure. They gave me their belief in tomorrow. I did not trust the Universe after Ronnie's death. Trusting in tomorrow was something I needed to borrow from them until I could regain the trust for myself. Phyllis and Mom added, *"Your life force is strong. You will get through this period in your life. All that you need to do is take the vitamins and minerals that you know are important for you."* They even mentioned Limu as a supplement, something I had never heard about before. Mom said, *"You have to take care of your blood pressure — because I said so!"*

When Mom was on this earth plane she would frequently use that phrase, 'because I said so.' That was the end of any discussion. I always knew when she was serious because she would give you one of her 'looks' or use that phrase. When our loved ones come through it is amazing how the exact phrases they used when they were in their physical bodies continue. Humor seems to be important to them. Many times when I was feeling challenged by a situation during our conversations they would add a funny phrase or grandiose statement to lighten up the discussion. It must be wonderful to be on the other side. They see and feel so much more than we can and simply want to be of help to us as we live out our own life script. I always felt better after hearing from them, just a little more in sync. It was as if my mental compass had been recalibrated to indicate true north and Polaris, the bright star almost directly above the North Pole guided me home. After hearing from them I felt the illumination from the five-point star was visible once again in my life and I had renewed strength to go on. Our families are always available to give us a loving reminder of what is important in life.

For those of us in the early stages of grief, we simply want to have our loved one back. We want to wake up tomorrow and discover that it was all a big mistake and they are not really gone. We miss them terribly and want them back, that's it! We aren't asking for too much, right? We are the parents or spouse or sibling that is left here and we feel we deserve to have our loved ones with us! I remember, so well, this period in the grief process. Three different times I actually thought I saw Ronnie from a distance — once at the picnic before his funeral that his friends from the Dolores Volunteer Fire Department had for us. Another time I thought I saw him walking across the street, and another time in a car. Each time would take my breath away. For a second I would think, maybe he isn't really gone, maybe it was a mistake — a cruel joke. Then I would remember the accident and the familiar heaviness in my heart would return.

Sadly, I have met people who do not even talk about their loved ones who have passed on. You feel like the topic is totally off limits — verboten — when they are around. Do they think that by not talking about them the pain of loss will be lessened? Why wouldn't you want to remember the loving moments you had with them? Or the times that would take your breath away with a joke they said that, in reflecting back, was so outrageous that you can actually laugh out loud today just thinking about it. My family members and close friends who have passed on are a frequent part of my conversations. I am not living in the past but honoring my loved ones who make my past, present and future that much better by staying connected with me through their unconditional love. I just figure if you don't want to hear about them don't listen — everyone has a choice. I have learned that I don't have to hold back my memories because it might make someone uncomfortable. People deserve to know how wonderful these people were in life and of the many ways they had a positive effect on others. A leading author talks about our children who are now in spirit and explains that they want so badly to continue to be a part of our lives. Each, in their own unique way, made a difference in this world and continue to do so from the other side. Now I understand what my mom meant when she said she would never be ready to say good-bye to me. You never say good-bye to unconditional love.

I also find it strange that some people actually believe that, 'once you're dead, you're dead, there is nothing else.' I know from experience that it is absolutely wrong-headed thinking. I believe these people are fearful and angry about so many things in life that their 'box' is not only closed with the lid securely fastened — it is encased in a vacuum packed seal. I actually had a person say those exact words to me about three weeks after Ronnie was killed. We had not been talking about Ronnie or anything remotely connected to the topic of death when she blurted out that statement. It took my breath away. The last thing you want to think about is that your child vanished without even the possibility of heaven or another plane of existence. If this person had stabbed me directly (rather than the indirect hit) in the heart it could not have been more hurtful. All I could manage to say, through clenched teeth, was, *"I don't share your belief and I don't ever want to talk to you about it again."* A few years later when she lost her own daughter, I wondered if the traumatic event caused her to question her nonbelief in God, the Universe or the Hereafter. Not having something greater than yourself to believe in must be a very cold, dark and lonely place to be.

Accepting the reality that I was going to write about my experiences, I met with Lee to discuss her ability to be a medium between both worlds. My quest was to find out what causes some people to receive information from the other side easier than others. Ronnie came through to tell me the following, *"You must sense when you can get information from the other side. It has to be an openness from the ones wanting the information. Their skepticism is simply doubt. When people are scared is shows in their body position. When you are working with someone who is fearful, the people on the other side just give Lee a little bit because they realize the person can't take very much. It's like an awareness on our side that some people really don't want to know. They just want to pass through life — they are insular. For some people spirituality is so frightening. Just try to get them to become more attuned — like the Dali Lama —to develop more self-awareness, and to find bliss in their life. People need to use balance and find their passion. Swimming, cooking, hiking, reading, or whatever they enjoy is important to do to bring more awareness to their life."* When you do something that you really enjoy, time feels like it is standing still. You relax and experience a different vibrational energy which opens you up to receiving nudges or messages from the other side. Ronnie continued, *"Even if they are reading this book, something is opening up to them. People love being in this energy. The conversation is happening.* <u>*Ninety percent*</u> *of our communication in our energy field* (on the other side) <u>*is used*</u> *to get through to people who are closed. Just plant the seeds in the book."*

He went on to say, *"You will help people lift the heaviness they feel. You are doing soul work. The lesson of balance is important for you too, Mom. It has to become a natural inclination from others to search for our truth. You have been preparing your whole life for this — you just didn't know it. Everybody in the family is behind this. Balance — remember the word — the world can consume a person. Have fun along the way. This book is more for people to hear how we have learned to connect so they can learn to do it too. As I have said, it is fun to talk with you through the writing. You hear me loud and clear!"*

My mom and sister came in then and said, *"We are here! This book will be like the last drop in the chalice that causes the water to overflow. It will be good to have some boundaries for yourself. You will be like a guide and you are taking people into this beautiful cave with a flashlight. But when you get to the cave you give them their own flashlight and say, 'Okay, now it's time for you to go in. You have the tools you need.'"* They went on to say, *"It will be important for people to think, 'why not, why not suspend judgment and just try it — let's take a journey together with this idea."* They added, *"Some people will never see it, it is not in their vibration. Some, however, will see it as a textbook, a talisman. You will give them the tools to go deeper and deeper into their own journey."*

When I heard Ronnie say that ninety percent of their energy is used to try to get through to people who are closed off to this type of connection, I realized I needed to do my part to try to help those folks who are hurting but not yet able to understand or believe in the possibility of spirit communication. Maybe reading about my experiences might help them find a greater level of peace.

After moving to Arizona, I visited Kartchner Caverns with a good friend. The caverns are unique since they are one of the few "living" caverns in the US. They are termed "living" because the mineral formations are still growing every moment due to the tiny drops of water within the caverns. It is absolutely breathtaking. Located in southeastern Arizona's Whetstone Mountains you could easily drive by what appears to be a medium sized hill (as compared to the Rocky Mountains) and miss everything. A hill is a hill is a hill — right? But that thought is, "Just wrong on so many levels" as my friend would say. Nothing in our world is "just" — it is a remarkable work of the Universe. Nature exists so that we can exist. What an amazing world we so often take for granted.

These caverns are an excellent analogy to our loved ones on the other side. You can just live life as you have known it — just drive by the cavern — or you can stop and go in, delve deeper and investigate what you don't know or haven't seen before and a whole new world of peace, love and connection will open up to you. The caverns, like our loved ones, may appear hidden from view, but are alive in spirit and waiting to communicate the love and beauty that surrounds them. You simply need to ready yourself by taking the time to investigate the possibilities, set your intention that the connection will happen and relax in the knowing that it will come to you in the exact time it is supposed to present itself. Your loved ones are waiting to be a helpful and supportive part of your life again. Don't keep your loved ones waiting.

After visiting the caverns, imagine my surprise when I replayed the CD from three years ago and heard my mom and sister give the example of the beautiful cave and my helping people find their own way to connect with the spirit world. The three of us had never been to a cave or cavern together. Synchronicity is indeed at work in everything we do. Many times I am so humbled by it and feel blessed to recognize and appreciate it for what it is — an assurance that the world, the universe is much bigger than our mere selves. We are like a grain of sand on a beach, important unto ourselves but not sufficient. It takes all of us together to make a beach, but it takes the immense power of the Universe to create the rhythmic rise and fall of the ocean tide that ultimately sustains us.

Water is a great analogy to consider when thinking about life. The oceans, lakes, rivers and streams are connected by physical properties, use and purpose. We can't always see where the water is flowing but it connects often in underground pathways then magically flows out of a mountain crevice to seek more of itself and join the larger flow of water from other locations. It is life giving and life sustaining and seeks something bigger than itself. We have our own internal use and purpose but seek the energy of others to add depth and meaning to our lives. We seek something bigger than ourselves to believe in and be a part of which are both life giving and life sustaining.

Through my losses in life I have become much wiser. I finally get what it means to "Let go and Let God, or the Universe." Previously, much of my life had been spent worrying about people, events, and things, basically just life in general. I now realize that it is wasted energy to worry and it blocks the positive elements coming to you. Now if I feel myself beginning to worry or doubt, I just say *"There is a reason for everything, a timing for everything and what is suppose to happen will happen, let it go."* I don't believe there are true mistakes in our lives. Lessons, of course! That's why we are here. Maybe there are even some 'oops,' moments or experiences when we went against our intuitive feelings and chose a different path. After all the good news is that we have the gift of free will. The bad news is, it is both a gift and a burden since only you are responsible for the decisions you make in life. You just can't blame them on anyone else. Ultimately, regardless of our choices, however, everything seems to happen for a purpose. When we begin to truly live by this belief, we experience an "Aha!" moment and know that there is so much more to appreciate and love and so very little to fear in life. Everything then becomes easier since it is more in line with what the Universe intends. You are swimming with the tide not against it. It takes less energy and gives more joy.

If a person can find a way to have more peace of mind through the trials and tribulations of life — I say take it! When I would go to Lee and she, as well as my family on the other side would say, *"You hear us and you can do this for yourself."* I knew that intuitively but just wanted the reassurance that I had an intermediary, so to speak, to help me hear more clearly and internalized the information with my head and my heart. I have now gained the faith that I can do this for myself.

Following up on Ronnie's explanation about why some people

seem to receive more information than others, I quizzed Lee to find out if she could channel for everyone. Does the process that works so well for me work universally? Her response was quite interesting and confirmed what Ronnie had told me. She said that if a person has a great deal of anger or fear around them, it impedes the communication. She explained that it is like a radio that is turned on but rather than hearing the words exactly she gets a great deal of static. She explained that she thought the static was due to an invisible wall of fear that was coming from and surrounding the person so the messages would sort of bounce off the wall and not get though as clearly. I mention this to you because you may have gone to someone and the information was either not on the mark or confusing at best. I heard a friendly skeptic say the other day, *"Oh, I don't believe in this kind of stuff. All those people tell you are basic generalizations that would apply to most people."* I hope that through my sharing of snippets from a decade of messages you realize that given a gifted medium, and assuming you do not have the fear that inhibits the communication flow, this type of communication is specific, relevant and just basically right on! Your loved ones are, in fact, communicating with you.

I specify "gifted" medium for a reason. I don't feel that all psychics, mediums or readers are able to achieve the same level of energy connection with you or with the other side. We all have our own skills and area of expertise. As in any other profession the art and skill involved in reading for others takes years to fully develop and perfect. I view it similarly to medical doctors, lawyers or educators. We all went to school for a prescribed period of time to earn a diploma but still have varying degrees of both talent and skill in our fields.

If you are in a city and see a sign that says, psychic readings — $10 — be careful — be very, very careful. Usually, they will give you a few generalized things and then say, "For $50 or $75 dollars more I can get into a much greater depth with you." Right, and I know of some swampland in Florida that's for sale! Remember the words, caveat emptor — let the buyer beware. Better to spend your money shopping. At least you will have the pleasure of something new to wear that is just drop dead gorgeous!

If you choose to contact a medium remember that it takes time for us who have lost a loved one to work through the initial steps in the grief process. Time allows us to gain perspective and calm which ultimately allows us to receive the most out of the reading. Be patient with yourself. Remember to have a little bit of faith, a little bit of courage and the desire to be mentally directed to a person who can help you begin to make the connections. Later on, as you gain more confidence and assurance in this bridge you will be able to make the connections yourself and be sure it is real.

To quiet your mind so that you can receive messages from the other side meditation is mentioned so much that it may seem obvious. Of the books I have read on spiritualism the use of meditation is recommended as well as prayer. I have read that prayer is really asking for something and meditation is more attuned to listening for something. The difference is an important one to consider. Lee, for instance, says a prayer before a session and asks only for information that is directed toward our highest good to come through and then she quiets herself and listens. Meditation is something that works, doesn't cost money and offers a greater sense of well-being. It seems as logical to me as prayer, just with a different intent. It is worth the effort to set aside even five or ten minutes per day to just relax and listen. Since it is too easy for me to get started on the day and then not stop to set aside time to meditate, I do this each morning before getting out of bed. I ask the Universe to surround me in white light and to be able to receive messages that are for my highest and greatest good. Then I simply wait a few minutes and listen. It helps me begin my day in a positive mindset and I am frequently both surprised and happy with what I 'hear.'

I realize that for some people who have recently lost a loved one their heart may feel like it is breaking and it may be impossible to relax into a meditative state. Just give yourself the gift of time but keep the goal out there to find your own way to meditate. Similarly when you are a super Type A personality, relaxing is simply a word pasted on the ceiling over your chiropractors' table. Seriously, does he really think reading the word will help? For me it just makes me more aware of the tightness of my muscles! However, you need to find your own unique way to relax. There is no prescribed way that works for all of us. You must do the work to discover what approach works best for you and enables you to hear and receive the communication from your loved ones. Maybe a walk in nature, yoga, or even cooking helps you get into the right emotional space. Discover and utilize whatever it is that that will stop the internal chatter in your mind and help you focus on hearing not thinking.

Neuroplasticity teaches us that our brain receives billions of bits of information per second much of which we discard and yet there are still approximately two thousand bits of information per second we actually process. We have over 3,000 complete thoughts with this information. It is no wonder that learning to slow down our thinking in order to meditate is a challenging and difficult task. For most of our lives we have been trying to do just the opposite — to speed up our thinking, reading and processing skills. Remember when multitasking was so in vogue? Well, meditation is the direct opposite to me. The goal is to slow down your own thought process and focus not on thinking but on hearing. It takes time to perfect but is definitely possible with practice. Breathe deeply and ask God or the Universe to help you discover the best approach to help you.

That is exactly what I do when someone is visiting me in Arizona and wants to go to a psychic or medium. I first suggest that they call Lee for an appointment. If they want to sit down immediately with a reader I just listen to them, slow down my thinking and let my brain process the request. I purposely let it go and wait for the answer. I don't force myself to come up with an immediate yes or no. Later on, I will either suggest we take a drive to Sedona (a mecca for the esoteric) or suggest we wait until their next visit. I have actually been in Sedona with a family member who wanted to stop when she saw a sign that read, "Psychic Readings –Walk-ins Welcome" and I just waited for the internal message to come. In a matter of a few minutes I said to her, "No, let's not stop there it just doesn't feel right." Was it the reader, the family member or the time that was the disconnect? I just don't know. I do know, however, that I have consciously taught myself to wait to receive an intuitive "go or no go" sign and then follow it. The next time this same family member came to visit and she wanted to connect with a reader, we drove to Sedona and everything just felt right. Although there were many shops advertising readings we just walked around and intuitively felt like stopping at a particular one. She went into the shop and connected with a very talented person. The timing was perfect. I humbly admit that there are things that are just way beyond my 'knowing' and I am finally okay with that. I have learned to trust God and the Universe and follow that lead.

When Lee continued to tell me I could do this for myself, I knew she was right but I didn't want to let go of our connection. She is an angel on earth and also a friend. She was right, however, to push me out of the nest. I had a book to write and, as a mom who lost her child, I needed to share my life with people and let them know they could actually reconnect with their loved ones. Just as I initially needed help in connecting I needed to explain the journey I followed to others. I know I couldn't have gotten to this point without the help of those two special people that God sent into my life at the perfect time. I was ready to receive help and needed to hear specifics from my son. I know now that I can do it for myself. Thanks guys!

As Ronnie said, "*Life can be its own gift or its own undoing.*" It all *revolves around developing one's consciousness about ourselves and about how unconditional love allows the communication from our loved ones to continue forever.*"

Thanks Ronnie, in addition to being my son, you have been my protector and guide. You have always been one-of-a-kind and I love you so much for it. I am glad to know that we will have eternity to be together.

Part III

Connections:
Coherence — Sequence — Continuity

If you look with your head and heart you will see:
Beyond chaos, there is a reason
Beyond darkness, there is light
Beyond absence, there is presence
Beyond nothingness, there are infinite possibilities
Beyond pain, there is healing
Beyond brokenness, there is wholeness
Beyond anger, there is peace
Beyond indifference, there is connection
Beyond boxes, there is infinity
Beyond questions, there are answers
Beyond silence, there is communication
With communication, there is love, light and peace

M.L.

Resolving Old Hurts

The edited conversations that I have shared with you from some of my recorded readings have been chosen for many reasons. First and foremost to show you how our loved ones want to remain an important part of our lives. You no longer need to feel hopeless or helpless. Our loved ones do not simply disappear. Their unconditional love is alive and well. They are waiting, patiently, for you to connect with them. They cannot do it alone. In any type of communication it takes both a sender and receiver. You need to do your part to make it happen.

I have also shared these with you to demonstrate how we can receive actual help, direction, reassurance and most importantly the continuance of their love as we progress on our own pathway in life. Further, I know that we can resolve any issue, receive forgiveness and achieve a deeper understanding from our loved ones if we humble ourselves enough to ask. Your earnest desire to work through and resolve any issue with your loved one can release the burden of loss, anger or guilt that you may be feeling. I know it is possible because I have asked for and heard their loving response.

The area of forgiveness is important for those of us on this earth plane.

Many of us have unresolved issues with a family member or close friend that has passed. We may go through life saying, 'if only I would have said this or that to them when they were alive.' If you have something that you simply cannot let go of and it is impeding your life lessons on this planet, then it is time to let it go! I know what you are probably thinking — right — easier said than done. I would respond to you, no it really is not easier said than done, for once it is said from the head and heart, it is done. Does that sound too simple? Well, it could be if you keep the thought in your head but don't feel it in your heart. Remember, once the head and heart connection is made and you recognize the continued existence of your loved one's spirit, the deep and everlasting RE-connection is made. If you can open yourself up to the possibility that what I have with my family on the other side is real then why would you not think that now is a perfect time for you to learn to make your own connection and release any burdens you may be carrying. Write down whatever it is that you wish you would have said or done to the person who has passed. Then relax, breath deeply and ask them to forgive you. We have all had family members who have gotten on our nerves to the point that we responded in a way that we were not proud of and consequently caused an alienation to develop. Someone needs to take the lead to mend the fences and say, "I'm sorry, please forgive me." Just because our loved ones are behind the door does not mean that a heartfelt apology cannot be asked for and received. Remember they are with us to help us and show their never-ending love. If they know something is impeding our healing don't you think they would want you to get passed it? You will be surprised by their loving response. I have learned the hard way that carrying around anger and allowing alienation to develop wastes the precious time we have with our loved ones on both sides of the door. The time wasted is just that — time that is needlessly squandered — gone forever.

It may be nearly impossible to understand the whole concept of this type of direct connection unless you have lost someone and it has affected you so deeply that it has changed you from the inside out. I get it because I have been there. I know, however, that once you are able to communicate with your loved ones you will see, "all is as it should be." Accepting that there is a God or universal consciousness or whatever label you choose to use to recognize a power greater than yourself, enables the connection to happen. You will find peace. Let these ideas rolls around in your brain for a while. A seed may be planted that your heart may encourage you to nurture and grow.

Think of the word 'hereafter.' We may hear it frequently but have you ever thought of it in a slightly different light? What does it really mean? The definition in Webster's New World Dictionary says, "from now on; in the future, following this, the state after death." Let's make our brains hurt a little here by really thinking about it. We were taught in grade school that when we are trying to understand a new word or concept after reading the definition we usually take it apart, pronounce it phonetically and think about how we can use it in our own setting. If we take this compound word apart what do we have — here and after. So ... just maybe ... the word hereafter as it was used historically really does mean the state of being here for ever after? Sure makes sense to me. I absolutely believe that our loved ones are here with us for ever after and are simply on a different vibrational level which makes seeing them difficult or impossible but still allows us to hear them. They are just waiting for you to open a channel to receive them. Mull it over until a truth becomes evident to you.

Gratitude is an important mindset to develop and maintain. It helps you surround yourself with positive energy. This not only causes you to feel better but enhances your ability to connect with your loved ones on the other side. I realize how hard it is to even think of being grateful for anything in life when you have lost a loved one. Time is the operative word here. It takes time to stop the bleeding of your heart. It takes time to accept the eventuality of your loss. It takes time to get through the devastating blow you have received in your life. A method that can help you get through these issues is to force yourself to think about five things everyday for which you are grateful. You may have to 'fake it until you make it' and feel a bit disingenuous at first. It's okay. I really do understand how challenging it can be, initially, to feel grateful.

Positive feelings of gratitude are indispensable to your healing. You may need to start with something basic such as the physical elements of water, light, air, the earth or your environment to begin saying and thinking of reasons to feel grateful. Your feelings may still be too raw to go into gratitude any deeper at first. Believe me, in Arizona during the summer when the temperature peaks at 117 degrees you can still be grateful for the beautiful light of the sun, the unique cacti that grow in the near drought conditions and the sunsets that are each more beautiful than the evening before. Everyplace we live on this earth has so many things for which to be grateful. We simply need to open our eyes to the beauty of the Universe that sustains us.

After you have practiced the five things you are grateful for in nature for a few weeks, move on to relationships. What are five things that you are grateful for in your relationships with family or friends? Who has made a point to check in with you to see how you are doing since your loss? Who has encouraged you to get out a bit, maybe to dinner or a movie? What cards or emails have you received that show you that others are thinking of you? The list could go on and on. Even though you may not feel like socializing at first, at least realizing that someone took the time to connect with you is important. That is a reason, in itself, to be grateful. Force yourself to stop and see the little things others do for you in the positive, loving light from which they were intended. After a few weeks of practicing both gratitude in nature and with others move on to the big one. Think of five things about your loved one who has passed for which you are grateful. What about them still brings a smile to your face when you think about it? Keep at this practice of gratitude daily. It will heal you in so many ways and will begin to break down the bricks in that wall of protection that you may have built around yourself after your loss. This is hard emotional work you are doing. Be patient with yourself if you slip up now and then and feel anger creeping back into your thinking. You are human it is natural. The road to healing is not a straight path, it has curves and switch backs along the way. The important think is to keep moving along the road. When you get into bed at night, close your eyes and review your gratitude list. You will be amazed as times goes on how much better you feel. Your loved ones on the other side want you to be happy. They need you to heal so they can reconnect and help you believe in tomorrow. Please don't disappoint them.

Existing Beliefs and Expanded Worldviews

I realize that I am asking you to change your concept of loss by considering possibilities that may be foreign to you. I am asking you to open the doors of your mind, even slightly. Your worldview has been created from your upbringing as well as everything you have done and learned to date. It is an amalgamation of your thinking and being. Some people hold on to their past understanding of life and death with a stranglehold. Nothing can change them. They are fearful to let go of 'what is' or what has been truth in their minds and consider the possibility of 'what could be.' Any change in our thinking, feeling or experiences initially creates a fear of the unknown, an uncertainty in our world. There are people who cannot handle change or uncertainty and choose to remain closed to new possibilities. Everyone has the right to exercise their own free will. Others can handle change more effectively. What I find intriguing are these people whose worldview continues to expand as they get older! They not only encourage change but celebrate it. They think about, observe and study different areas that are unknown to them. Little by little, their perceptions and subsequent worldview becomes bigger, greater, just more of everything. How wonderful it is to run across people who are less fearful and more inquisitive about the big questions in life. These are the people who are often sought out as good friends or simply people we enjoy being around because they are interesting, upbeat and full of possibilities. They are ongoing learners on this earth until the day they take their last breath. Just being around them makes you feel better. Their insight is keen and their hearts are open to possibilities regardless of their age or life experiences. The energy they emit is so powerful that you feel more positive and invigorated just being in their presence.

Speaking of their energy, remember you can't necessarily see it right? But you can feel it and you know those special people who help you have a more upbeat outlook. You could probably name them right now. Unfortunately, you could also name the people you try to avoid being around because they are negative thinkers and basic naysayers about life. We feel drained just being in their presence. If you can relate to this idea of energy why would it be so difficult to think of energy on a spiritual sense? Energy is energy. It may not be able to be seen but it can be felt. So why is ongoing communication with our loved ones who have passed on such a difficult concept to accept or believe in? Could it be fear? Remember the statement made by Franklin D. Roosevelt in his 1933 inaugural address, 'there is nothing to fear but fear itself'? Although he was referring to the economic times at the moment, that phrase could be applied to everything we do in life. It truly applies in this context.

Our loved ones who have passed on are no longer controlled by fear. Ronnie has explained to me that after the body — the shell — is finished, the learning continues. The light of knowledge and greater understanding has illuminated the darkness. The ability to see and understand is so much greater for our loved ones than when they were walking on this earth. Doesn't it make sense to recognize their greater capacity and ask for help, love, guidance maybe even forgiveness from the people who you loved so dearly? If unconditional love is truly unconditional, and in physics we know that energy cannot be created nor destroyed only changed in form why wouldn't it make sense to connect the dots and connect with them?

Our beliefs are powerful things. They were not formed overnight and won't be changed overnight. Any door to your mind can be opened or closed. People can receive greater peace through a deeper understanding or continue to live in anger, fear or depression The choice is always up to us. It will take work to change your present belief structure and even more work to create a larger one that incorporates a belief in communication with the other side and no one else can do it for you. I would just challenge you to consider an expanded worldview, one that includes the love, help and guidance that the universe, through our loved ones, has to offer.

I have always been a huge proponent of seeking answers to the big questions in life. I expect to continue this quest for the rest of my life. I choose to expand my understanding of the other side not only because of the guidance and love connection I feel, but because I want to share this with people who are so weighed down by grief that they have stopped truly living. The light or spark has gone out of their lives. Just by looking in their eyes you can see that they have experienced a loss that has rendered them nearly helpless. Grief is so prevalent in all of our lives. However, it is something most of us are totally unprepared for and we simply try to muddle through it. I know that it does not have to be this way. In fact, it should not render us helpless.

Let me ask you this, if you haven't thought about ongoing communication with a loved one on the other side, what do you have to lose? Please disregard the ideas and feelings that are conjured up in our minds from the TV programs or movies that use scary music and frightening scenes to capture the interest of the viewer. Fear seems to be a big seller in the marketplace. I have read that many people want to be entertained with something fearful because they have so much fear in their own lives. I don't understand that type of rationale. It seems so sad. Times are, indeed, tough but playing on the fear of individuals may help the station's ratings or movie profits but doesn't do much to give a person confidence to delve into the bigger questions in life in search of greater peace. What I can tell you, with certainty, is that I have never heard of anyone who was fearful *after* experiencing communication of this type. In fact, it is quite the opposite. Open lines of communication dispels the fear and allows us to live more fully.

To keep myself centered and surrounded with positive energy and to eliminate any effect from the negative energy from others I make it a habit of saying the following when I am meditating, around a negative person or atmosphere and before going to sleep at night:

> May the pure white light of Christ's consciousness be
> my protector and guide so no evil will harm me or neg-
> ative will affect me and I will love everyone. I choose to
> live my life in the white light of peace, joy and love.

It helps me to remind myself that some people or situations can be an energy drain and it is not my job to try to make them feel better. Of course, I will continue to be empathetic to someone who is experiencing a problem but not to those people who just want to perseverate in their 'poor me' attitude. I will no longer allow that to affect me. It is not healthy for me and I'm not sure how good it is to enable them to continue their energy drain on others. When people regularly use you to 'dump' their stuff, it slowly and insidiously buries you under a mountain of their yuk. I have enough of my own stuff to work through, thank you. I don't need to shoulder the burden of someone else's negative energy. Besides, if there is a pile of yuk, I want a pony or horse to be in it. It takes work to keep a positive attitude. You can't simply buy a stamp for your hand that signifies 'only positive thinking is allowed around me' and expect it to happen. That would be way too easy. No, it has to be a conscious choice to stay in the positive thought process and one that you must work at daily. I can see the difference in people who choose the positive over negative and so can you. It has to take more energy to be in a negative mindset, just look at the faces of those people. They look tired, depressed, and angry — because they are choosing it! I don't understand why — maybe I am not supposed to for now.

To connect with our loved ones on the other side you must — absolutely must — rid yourself of the negative energy in your environment. If you are immersed in a life sapping environment you are not only hurting yourself but being complicit as others drain you of your precious life force. If someone is dumping on you regularly — stop them — you can no longer afford it if you want to create the ongoing communication with your loved ones behind the door.

So what is preventing us from making the connections with our loved ones? In addition to the fear factor, does the whole idea sound too preposterous to be true? So was the idea of taking a trip to the moon in 1950. Now we take space travel for granted. Or how about the thought that "others" will think you have lost your grip? Well, that is always a risk but it is one I am willing to take for the reward. Besides, have you ever noticed that many people who do not want to talk about things like this are also pretty closed in other parts of their lives? They remind me of the saying, don't confuse me with the facts; or what can be even more threatening to them, don't confuse me with something that appears intangible. Really? Love can be intangible and yet we know it when we see it or feel it right? If you haven't experienced this type of communication I realize that just reading this book may not be sufficient for you to believe it is possible. It is the actual experience of hearing the words, communicated in their own unique way from your loved one that creates believers.

The grief process is the most devastating thing a person can go through. I read that the depth of your loss is directly related to the depth of your love. When you lose a child, a parent, a sibling, partner or spouse that you have loved unconditionally the gut wrenching begins, as we know. How do we stop it? Do we just think that time will heal your broken heart? There are songs written about healing a broken heart but I don't think that time alone is enough. I feel that the heart might heal over but will leave scar tissue because you have lost a piece of your life. You have lost someone that made life real to you and gave your life greater purpose. Maybe it was someone that was your protector or the one person you could go to and trust them to listen and care. Even more devastating, maybe it was the child that when you think of them you can remember their first breath, first steps, their first every thing. When you lose this significant person in your life all the stages of grief come crashing in on you. It is as if we are in a maze with no ending.

Two months after my son was killed, my eleven-year-old son asked me one day, "Are you ever going to be like my Mom again?" If that doesn't create a wake up call to a mother, I don't know what will. I did my best to get my act together. I attempted to hide the scar tissue in my heart but it was just below the surface, always with me. Those of you who have been through this know the next sentence before I write it. When I was by myself, the tears would come and I would be right back to the stage of, *"Why, why, why did this have to happen?"* If there is a way then to make it more bearable, doesn't it make sense to consider it?

Some of you may have a 'wait and see' attitude about the concept of this type of communication. That is understandable. A good dose of skepticism in life is a good thing if it causes us to investigate further. If it shuts down our thinking or causes us to remain in our box or our fear — oblivious to possibilities, we might want to stop and reassess. Choose to grow in faith and love; not sink in the stagnation of fear or anger.

I know that our loved ones are just behind the door as Ronnie has said many times to me since his passing. Initially finding someone to connect with him was my life raft. I needed assurance that when thoughts would literally pop into my head that reflected the love, protection even humor that he was noted for, it was really him. I wanted to be sure that I wasn't making it up in a desperate attempt to hold on to my son. I needed someone who could connect all the dots for me. I can now discern when a thought pops into my head and is phrased in a certain way, if it's my son, mom or sister. I have finally arrived at the stage that I know the difference between my own organized, planned and logical type of thinking and something that resembles a nudge or a thought that seems to come out of nowhere. I have also learned how to recognize and appreciate the synchronicity of events that happen that are tender messages from my loved ones.

Synchronicity is an incredible way to realize the power that exists to help us in our journey though life. It took time to get to the point of recognizing it and knowing how to utilize it in my life. It's a simple idea that is complex in reality. Basically, we are given the opportunity to tap into the higher consciousness for help, ideas, relief from the pain of loss, or anything else for our greater good. We simply need to put our positive intentions out there by stating our absolute belief in attaining them and then patiently let go and watch for the subtle indicators that indicate a direction — a confirmation to guide us. For example, most of us have experienced thinking of someone and the phone rings and it's that person. What do you think causes this to happen? Jung's classic work, 'Synchronicity: An Acausal Connecting Principle' explains that it is a coincidence of events, that involves more than the mere probability of chance being involved. OK, so what *is* that something? I believe it consists of three distinct elements: a belief that it is possible, a positive intention or desire and a connection made with your mind energy that allows the Universe to manifest your request or desire. You give it to the Universe as a positive request and allow the response to happen. I no longer perseverate about it but just trust in the proper timing of the Universe. Going back to the example of the phone call, you were probably thinking about the person about the time they decided to call. I believe your thoughts or theirs were transferred to the other person and through the energy of the thoughts a message was sent and received. When you are emotionally close to someone we sometimes refer to that as being on the same wavelength. I experience this with my family on both sides of the door. It happens regardless of distance or dimension. There are many excellent books that explain how to tap into the power of coincidence or synchronicity.

The three elements of belief, intention and connection are the keys to establishing communication with our loved ones who have passed on. You have to believe that it is possible and want and expect it to happen, be in a positive state of mind and then relax in the knowing that the Universe will provide if it is for a higher intention. Hopefully, my years of documented discussions with my loved ones will cause you to at least entertain the possibility of it being real and you will be encouraged to make your own connections. My intention is that given the unconditional love that I share with my family our communication is always for the highest good for all concerned. My connection, therefore, is unbroken. I have a belief in the possibility and the positive intention of helping self and others with the information I receive. My connection to my son is like a circle of love that will always be unbroken. As Ronnie has told me it represents infinity just as the Universe represents infinity.

According to research a majority of people believe in some form of higher power and use various names or titles that are comfortable to them. Some have strong connections to a traditional dogma and religion. I was raised a Catholic, that is to say, my mother was Catholic and my dad an atheist. That gave me a rather wide berth for study and investigation.

I was attending a public high school and enjoying it for the most part. My grades were good, cheerleading was excellent (that was back in the dark ages when there were no other sports for girls to be involved in) and being on the Homecoming court made school life pretty sweet. However, my mother, being a woman of few words decided that it would be good for me to attend Nazareth Academy, a Catholic High School for girls for my junior and senior years. Her rationale was that since I had not attended catechism classes for the past six years it would be a good experience. I really think she decided that boys — or at least one boy was becoming a little too important in my life. All I can remember saying is, *"Nazareth, isn't that a Catholic girls' school?"* Mom gave me a one-word answer, *"Precisely."* End of discussion. It was next announced that I wouldn't need any new school clothes that year since I would be wearing uniforms!

Uniforms! Are you with me on this — sixteen-years old and having to wear navy blue A-line skirts, white, blue or pink blouses, a white blazer or blue sweater and saddle shoes! All of these items had to be purchased through the same supplier to assure regulation attire. The operative word here is 'regulation' a point I missed early on in my experience. I couldn't decide which one of those items of dress were worse. They were not even showing saddle shoes in catalogues. Where in the world did you find such ugly things? There was no discussion, pleading or arguing with my mother. All you needed was "the look" to send shivers down your spine.

Trying to make the best of a difficult situation, I drove my boyfriends' convertible, top down, radio blaring, onto the long, tree-lined drive on the first day of school and was greeted at one of the four parking spaces available by Mother Superior. She gave me a steely once over and informed me that I was to put the top up and turn the radio off before turning onto the property. I was not stupid and quickly realized this was going to be an interminably long year. At least I was able to live at home and attend day school rather than live on campus. However, this put me totally out of touch with anyone from my old school but the one boy I had been dating since ninth grade. I wanted to point this out to Mom, but I thought it would not go over well. Her plan had really backfired. Rarely was my mother ever wrong about my life. Reflecting back over the past six plus decades, I believe this was the one and only time. If only I had been smart enough to understand how clearly she could see.

Attending this school was totally foreign territory to me. I had so many questions and no one seemed willing or able to supply the answers. For instance, I often wondered if any of the nuns noticed that when the girls who lived on campus during the week went home on the weekends, they always ended up in the confessional booths on Monday mornings before Mass. Another thing that puzzled me was why we had to use the back stairs as juniors? I asked — I thought this was a democracy — and the answer was, of course, that it was a privilege to use the front stairs that was only awarded to the higher-ranking seniors. I tried to point out the flawed logic — there were, at most, a total of twenty-five girls in each grade and traffic jams did not happen on the front stairs. My boldness at even questioning the tradition was gently but firmly pointed out. Frequently, I ran late and would run up the senior stairs to get to class. Occasionally, around the corner and out of view at the top of the staircase, would be Mother Superior. I swear she had a homing device on me. I would be directed to the office to give her one of the fifteen honor beads from my necklace. The necklace was regulation attire as well — not to be confused with a fashion statement — beads were not even 'in' at the time. Finally after losing at least half of them — due to either the stairs issue or the 'unladylike' behavior of crossing my legs in class, I was called to her office once again to give up another bead. You guessed it — the stairs again. She must have been an alien who had eyes not only in the back of her head but secretly implanted in a 360-degree pattern underneath her veil. A truce was drawn. I politely suggested that she just keep the rest of the beads and I would commit to using the stairs only in a severe emergency. She agreed and we had an arrangement that worked well for the rest of the year.

During my year at Nazareth, I remember asking the nun who was teaching religion classes if a person could get to heaven if they were not Catholic. This was back in the early 1960's when many practices and teachings of the church were even more strict than today. I thought her answer was fascinating. She responded, "Yes, I believe they could but I do think it would be harder." Well, that worked for me at the time. I had already decided that if she said no, it would be hypocritical for me to stay and pretend to believe in that dogma. I knew too many wonderful people who were not Catholic to accept that there was only one way to get to heaven. To me, the need to 'check your Catholic pass' at the gates of heaven before being admitted just seemed too bizarre to be true. No, I reasoned to myself, I would just have to leave and try to reason with my mom later as to why. I'm still not sure how it happened but at the end of the year I received the award for the, "Most Improved Student in Religion." My best friend at school literally fell out of her chair and on to the floor laughing, when it was announced. Seriously, it's not that I didn't appreciate the honor but it was based on studying a small book on the lives of famous saints of the church. The chapter format was predictable and the testing was simply knowledge based — no analysis or synthesis thinking — what a surprise. Reviewing the material I could see that is was so easy that I thought if I could take the religion class in an independent study format I could remain in my French class and avoid the time conflict in my schedule. I had always been a hard worker and was more than willing to do more now by taking the extra class. Mother Superior wouldn't budge on this one. Sadly, after my first year of Latin in the public school, my second year of a foreign language in high school never transpired. I did a double take on this decision. I could not understand why a student wouldn't be encouraged to do more not less if they truly wanted to push themselves. I felt like I was wearing two left saddle shoes the entire year. Consequently, in the spring of my junior year, I calculated the course credits that I had accrued in my first three years in high school. I realized that I had enough credits to graduate a year early if I simply took one more English class at the Junior College over the summer. I thought I might have a chance with this proposal to Mother Superior since she was the only nun who plucked her eyebrows — a very progressive sign at the time. She seemed to be as glad as I was when I requested permission to take the summer class and graduate a year early.

I realized then that asking the big questions in life or questioning arbitrary rules was rarely valued by others. It usually just made them uncomfortable. Conformity was valued, individuality — not even close. It took Mother Superior about fifteen seconds to give her approval! I took English 101, applied the college credit to high school and graduated in August with a job waiting. My part-time job morphed into a full time one and I was confident I had made the right decision for me.

I have been seeking answers, challenging mindsets and endorsing change ever since my experience at Nazareth. The time spent there was valuable. I saw the full range of open and closed thinking in an organization and the difference one person can make to a life. I lived simultaneously both the constraints and joys in the familiar. All of these experiences confirmed what I felt driven to do. I choose to investigate, study and continue to seek a higher level of understanding about anything in life that crossed my path. There is so much to learn and the more we learn the more we appreciate the wonders of our Universe. It just seems to me that while we are on this planet there are so many big issues to learn more about — like what is the meaning of life? I mean, really, haven't you ever wondered that from time to time? Or here's another, do you really think it is possible for one person, institution or belief to have it all figured out perfectly? This would make them the sole purveyor of absolute truth. How in the world is that possible? I question if anyone, anyplace on this earth plane could be that all-knowing.

I prefer to think about a hybrid approach to a belief system. One in which we look at the essential commonalities rather than the differences. I prefer a belief system that encourages me to question, seek answers and accept responsibility for my own actions in life. An inclusive system that values all individuals because they are a piece of the divine in the Universe is important to me. Certainly, everyone has a right to their own belief system, even atheists. They in particular will have a wonderful surprise coming after they pass on. If you have something that works for you — excellent! If it energizes you and makes you feel loved and less fearful about life then you are in the right place. I would simply suggest that in keeping with the idea of enlarging your worldview and continuously learning as an individual you might want to keep yourself alert to the possibilities of integrating even more possibilities into your belief system as you continue to learn, grow and become the unique individual you were destined to be. Think of the beauty of a hybrid rose, it makes other roses dull by comparison.

Communicating with those who have passed on is frequently not on the radar screen with more established religions. Why, I'm not sure. I don't see it as a competition about who is right. For me it is not in conflict with believing in a higher power or energy source. After the past decade of having these communications with my son and mother and seven years with my sister how could I question the legitimacy? What I do know is that it takes faith in a higher power, and a humbling of one's ego to realize that this communication is possible. Unconditional love is never ending. The chain really is unbroken; we just may not be able to physically see all the links.

Self-help books abound with emphasis on the strength of practicing positive beliefs, visioning, meditation and, of course, prayer. They emphasize the importance of surrounding yourself with people that make you feel better when you are with them and they give examples, of course, of the opposite — the energy drainers who consistently see their cup as half empty. The operative word here is 'consistently.' We all have days when we aren't at our best and need someone to listen to us as we recap our latest trials and tribulations. Once again, you couldn't see the actual energy draining from you or conversely you couldn't see the positive energy from others actually going into your energy field, right? But you can feel the result. Well, don't you wonder what exactly it is that you feel? How can this happen? When you read the paper about all the negatives happening in this world doesn't it make you feel heavier, sad or frustrated? It certainly does me. We may not be able to see our energy field change but we certainly can feel it. We simply know it happens and don't need visual proof since we have experiential truth.

When we talk about other emotions such as love, acceptance, denial, anger, even hate (a word I dislike immensely), those are simply words, but they elicit emotions in your body. I think if we could measure the energy sapping capacity of the word, hate, it would be off the chart! You can feel it. It is a word that causes me to wince just hearing it. Well, I ask you again, if you can't see it how can you know what it really is or that it even exists? In goal setting, we learn that words trigger emotions on the subconscious level. These emotions then affect your behavior. Basically your behavior is the result of the feelings and emotions that you have allowed in your consciousness. It is important to be aware of the words you use, the experiences you choose to be involved with as they will become a natural part of your thinking in the future. Words and emotions are powerful things since they change our energy field. Most of you who have had children and have experienced the feeling of the unconditional love of your child would respond, "I just KNOW it is real, I feel it." Of course you do. It may be something you can't really see or touch but you know that it exists.

Well, let's combine these thoughts. If we believe in something like love and can feel it just by thinking about someone we care about deeply, we have already learned how to allow ourselves to suspend our need to 'see it to believe it' right? And if we have chosen to lead a more positive, truthful, fulfilling life, and eliminate as many negative people or situations as possible, we have chosen to be in control of our life and to make things happen rather than let things happen to us.

Why would it be so difficult to believe in something else you can't see or touch but you can feel? When our loved ones pass on, we can no longer see them or touch them but if we are in a positive, prayerful or meditative state of mind we can communicate with them. They are patiently waiting for us to believe it possible and make the connection.

Extraordinary Researchers

There have been a multitude of interviews conducted and books written by Elisabeth Kübler-Ross during her career. Some of her thoughts, particularly in the early 1980s, were quite enlightening for the time and have now become more accepted as truth. She spent her life working with people who were dying. Trying to help them understand the stages involved in the dying process as well as attending to their physical and emotional needs as they progressed along their pathway. Early in her career she did not elaborate on her feelings about the possibility of the other side but rather devoted herself to establishing the importance of surrounding the dying patient with peace, love and in as little pain as possible. Thanks to her insights, the Hospice movement has made tremendous gains and is a viable option for well over one million people yearly in the U.S. Hospice care includes the physical, emotional, spiritual and social needs of the patient. In 2009 there were 3,364 hospice organizations around the country that were recognized for their significant contribution to allowing people to die with dignity and in the comfort of their own surroundings. Pain is managed according to the doctor's recommendations combined with the wishes of the patient and family. The Hospice organizations give palliative rather than curative care to the patient and emphasize the quality rather than the mere quantity of the days, weeks and months they have remaining. The bereavement services they offer to the families of the patients who have passed on are important to the over all quality of life for the survivors.

In addition to her work with Hospice, Dr. Kübler-Ross referenced in her writing the thousands upon thousands of cases that she personally witnessed of death and the near death experience that caused her to expand her thinking (developing a hybrid in her system of belief) about the other side. I have mentioned the five stages of death that she developed: denial, anger, bargaining, depression, and acceptance. I believe when we lose a loved one, we experience the same stages as those who are departing this earth. The length of time in the stages can vary greatly with each individual but we will all experiences those stages.

She learned through her work with dying patients the need to eliminate any negative feelings or emotions that we may be carrying around in order to achieve greater energy and peace of mind. This thought applies to all of us, not only to the dying. Most of us can remember negative experiences from our childhood. Things that physically or emotionally hurt, frightened or embarrassed us. If you think about these negative emotional experiences over and over they are recorded in your mind as a new reality. It's as if the same issue has happened to you hundreds or thousands of times. This adversity that you faced as a child (or adult) can be visualized as rocks in the backpack that you are carrying through life. By holding onto the negative memories, you become pessimistic about tomorrow and expect (and attract) more problems in your daily life. It is a vicious circle. Since we become what we think about most often, we literally fall into a habit of negative thinking and consequently create more negative experiences in our lives. Remember the saying, 'like attracts like' it is apropos here. Our backpacks continue to grow heavier. We must rid ourselves of these negative memories since they are not helping but actually hurting us. The Universe just seems to have a way of providing to us what we think about most often — be it negative or positive. Write the negatives on a piece of paper, review them, and be aware of how they make you feel. Then choose to tear up, burn or simply throw the paper away and let the negative memories dissolve into nothingness. Mentally throw the issues away as you physically discard the torn paper. Look at those pieces of paper as bricks that have been surrounding you with negative energy and sabotaging your belief in a more positive tomorrow. They restrict your energy flow leaving you tired, depressed or angry. Accept the belief that although they once were, they are no more. You have the power to cast them aside and live a more joyful life. As with all negative memories, the sad or hurtful memories you have of the death of your loved ones are not serving any good purpose and instead are keeping you in limbo between what was and what you wished could have been. When you find yourself momentarily reflecting back on these negative experiences from you list redirect your thoughts. Say to yourself, 'stop dwelling on the negative experiences of the past, let them go' and force yourself to remember at least one good memory from the past. Practice makes perfect with this approach. It takes time to redirect your thinking so that you are in a more positive mindset the majority of the time. Remember the saying, 'Let go and let God.' Dr. Kübler-Ross has suggested screaming at the top of your lungs in your car or house, or beating a pillow to rid yourself of this baggage. Discover something that works for you that can bring those deep-seated feelings of hurt and anger to the surface so they can be subjected to the healing power of the light of day. Don't risk developing a physical malady from something that has happened to you in the past — even yesterday — better to recognize the negative for what it is — a negative that has rocked your world and doesn't seem fair. When we lose a loved one, especially our child, it really doesn't seem fair or right. We are older, the parent and in the natural order of things would be expected to pass on first. We want to rail at the unfairness of it all. As a parent our job is to protect our child, and yet, we didn't. I understand. As difficult as it is we must even view this life altering tragedy, something that you can't undo by dwelling on it, for what it is — a terrible tragedy that cannot be reversed. As much as we want to change the facts in our heart the reality of what happened is immutable. After grieving your loss for a reasonable time you must force yourself to move on with your life. Even if you have to pretend you are better — just do it — and gradually you will be able to move on into the light and love that you had with that person. Dr. Kübler-Ross proposed in the 1980s what we now know to be true — when you hold on to or bury negatives in your psyche, illness is often a result.

Since it is impossible to hold simultaneous divergent emotional thoughts in your mind (for example, a negative and positive about the same event) which type of emotion would you choose to fill up the spaces in your mind and heart? Which approach would the loved one that has passed on choose for you? Negative, emotionally draining, fear-based thoughts or positive energy gaining thoughts of possibilities? You can observe the way people walk, talk, sit or stand and clearly see how much emotional baggage they are carrying around. Fear and anger are the real leveling agents in all of our lives. Regardless of the wealth you possess they can render you helpless with indecision and paralyzed with disbelief in a better tomorrow. Fear is heavy, dark and drains the life force right out of you. Choose to let go of the fear and anger from your loss and embrace the light and love that we are all capable of feeling. Love is the most powerful, healing force in the Universe. It is light, it is energizing and it allows us to make the connections between our worlds and our loved ones who have passed on.

Elaborating on her life work with Hospice, the dying patients and the development of the stages of dying, Dr. Kübler-Ross made the clear distinction between grief and grief work. It is important to know the difference. Grief itself is an intense and emotionally gripping state of being. It can cause the strong to buckle and the proud to bend. We learn resiliency, however, when we face the painful reality of illness and death. There is nothing easy about living through the grief brought on from the loss of a loved one. You can't escape the time and effort that is needed to get through it. Finding someone to care enough to listen to you as you relive the life experiences of your loved one will help. Someone that will listen to you in a way that you have never been listened to before. Talking through your grief, over time, is healing.

Think of a physical injury, it takes time to heal. Similarly, an emotional injury takes time to heal just as certainly as your bones take time to heal. You can't just pretend it doesn't exist and move on. As difficult as it is you need to process through your loss. If not, the toll that denial takes on your total being is frightening. Denial seems to create festers in our minds which fill with bitterness and insidiously take hold in our psyche. You will have to deal with your grief, sooner or later. It is important to see it for what it is -- an emotional injury -- that you will heal from given enough time and belief in the tomorrows of our lives. Healing does not mean to forget your loved one, but rather to honor them by becoming physically and emotionally healthy again as you move through your life. Basically, you just have to put one foot in front of the other and keep going even with your broken heart. I know it is tough, remember I speak from experience not simply theory.

Grief work, on the other hand, is when you have feelings of guilt or shame attached to the feelings of grief. The more you think about the loss the worse you feel. You can't seem to control the constancy of your thoughts or the feeling of self reproach as they flood into your mind. It can cause you to feel as if you are in a no-win situation, a vicious cycle, and unable to find a way out. For instance, you may feel badly about things that you did not do for your loved one who was dying or feel shame about something you said or didn't say to them before they died. I know that I have heard from family members who have been totally exhausted both mentally and physically and just wanted the dying process with their loved one to be over. They felt guilty saying it but they were at the end of their rope. Regrets are understandable but guilt and shame are not. Everyone could think about something else they wished they would have said or done for their loved one before they crossed over. If you are experiencing guilt or shame regarding how you responded during their stages of death it is time to let it go. At the time, you did everything you could do in the situation. Was it enough? Was it all you could do? It probably was at the time. I would find it difficult to believe that you are reading this particular book if you had not done everything you could have at the time of their death. Would you have done something differently in retrospect? Possibly, but remember, hindsight is always twenty/twenty. We must live life forward and our vision is not always twenty/twenty. We do our best with what we have at the time. No more, no less. The point is not to beat yourself up with the should have's and could have's. Allowing yourself to hold on to the guilt or shame is emotionally and physically debilitating and a waste of the time God or the Universe has given you on this earth. No one is perfect. Any one of us could go back and wish something — anything — could have been done differently. Forgiving yourself for being human is what it is all about. Your loved ones want you to let it go. You owe it to them to do so. Seeking professional help to work through your grief may be necessary and invaluable.

Earlier in this book, I suggested another way to approach healing if you are in the grief work stage. Yes, it involves talking, sharing and crying with others if you so choose, but also includes doing so directly with the loved one who has passed on. At first, you might try writing it all out and asking for understanding, forgiveness or help. Another approach is to find a reputable medium who can channel your loved one so that you can hear their response through another person. Later on as your acceptance grows and you are working from a point of knowing that they are just behind the door, a straightforward conversation with them will be possible. I found that what I felt I had not 'delivered on' with a family member ended up not to be an issue to her at all. For example, in 1985 my sister said she wanted to move out to Colorado and live with me. She had talked frequently about moving but never seemed ready to risk the unknown. Rather than help her make the transition to Colorado, I choose, instead, to get remarried. I had always felt guilty over it. During one of our conversations since her passing, my sister said to me, *"Will you please get over it! It wasn't suppose to happen that way or it would have. I am not angry with you."* Please reread the last sentence once again. My sister said the same thing that your loved ones would say to you. They do not hold onto grudges or issues on the other side. They are above and beyond that type of behavior. 'It happened as it was suppose to happen.'

It helped me to understand the three stages involved in the actual death process. The first stage is the physical stage when you lose consciousness and your brain ceases to function. The second stage is the psychic stage in which you have total awareness of events around you. Ronnie explained this stage to me when he said he could see Gina trying to resuscitate him but that he wasn't alone. An older male figure was with him and surrounding him with love. The third stage is when you are out of you body and time and space no longer exists. Ronnie confirmed this to me by saying he can be with his loved ones, here and on the other side, simply with a thought. The challenges of time and space are no longer constraints for our loved ones. He is like a butterfly that has shed the cocoon — the body — that he was in and is free of the weight of a physical body. Ronnie said that when we die we are totally surrounded by love and our family and friends who have preceded us in death. We are never alone. He added that he feels totally nurtured with the unconditional love that surrounds him. The picture he gave me in my mind helped me, immensely, as his mother.

I believe that we do have guardian angels or spirit guides who are with us from birth through our entire life and actual death of our bodies. They choose to be with us on our life journey as we learn our lessons. When our lessons are learned, our spirit, our soul is allowed to soar. When we stop letting the fears in life and especially surrounding the issue of death occupy our minds, we can then give more of our body and mind to healing ourselves — from the inside out.

Data indicates that twenty to thirty percent of the world's population believes in reincarnation regardless of their religious background. The belief was an integral part of church doctrine as early as the fifth century B.C. and continued through the early teachings of the Christian church (553 A.D.). In fact, although there were frequently other religious controversies, the issue of reincarnation was viewed as fundamental dogma and never challenged during this entire period. The story of how it ended is eye opening and demonstrates how absolute power corrupts absolutely. Reincarnation was eliminated during the reign of the Byzantine emperor, Justinian. His concubine turned wife, Theodora, of questionable background wanted total power over the people of the region. She did not want people to continue thinking that they were responsible for their own destiny. In 527 A.D. Justinian and Theodora represented the Imperial Crown, the Eastern Roman Empire, which was the highest power in the secular world. However, worldly power was not enough for Theodora. She desired deification or godly status after death and a physical place permanently designated for her remains within the church walls. She knew that she couldn't enter eternity as a goddess if the belief continued to be supported by the church that everyone returns to earth as mere mortals and are ultimately accountable for their transgressions. She manipulated the power within the existing church structure and replaced the Pope who had continued to support reincarnation as a basic tenant of church doctrine with Virgilius. This newly appointed Pope was complicit in his actions to support her wishes to eliminate reincarnation in church doctrine. At her urging he dissuaded the clerics particularly from the Western Churches who supported reincarnation from attending the Ecumenical Council meeting where the vote was taken to eliminate all references to reincarnation. The Synod of the Eastern Church of Constantinople subsequently revoked the affirmation of reincarnation from the church doctrine. Theodora was then successful in her quest to be deified as a goddess for all eternity and thus not accountable for her malevolent earthly actions.

Numerous religions of the world believe in reincarnation. It is an intrinsic element of many Native American traditions as well. The Dalai Lama once said, if science can disprove reincarnation Tibetan Buddhism would subsequently abandon it as well. Interestingly, he added, it would be 'mighty hard, however to disprove.' Remembering the first law of thermodynamics we know that energy can not be created nor destroyed, only changed in form. To me reincarnation is that change in form.

I believe that we do continue to reincarnate in physical bodies as we work on the lessons we choose to learn in each lifetime. I do not find this in conflict with existing belief structures. I would define my belief as a Practicing Spiritual Christian. Whether you choose to wrap your mind around the topic of reincarnation or not, I would suggest that you read more on the topic before deciding. I just know the energy of our loved ones changes form but it is never destroyed.

I mentioned synchronicity earlier and must demonstrate at this juncture. While writing about the stages of loss and the critical importance of surrounding yourself with positive energy, I had two amazing things happen to me at the precise moment they were needed. I had signed up for a workshop on holistic healing at the Banner Del Web Hospital in Surprise, Arizona. This hospital is doing amazing things with music (the healing melodies of harps), pet therapy, aromatherapy, and so much more. Just to hear that a medical facility is searching for every way possible, setting aside the purely traditional "in the box" thinking, to assist their patients in healing was exciting. This organization is on the cutting edge (no pun intended) of breakthroughs in the healing process and is proud of it! Thank you to all of the pioneers out there who are making this a reality. I expected a maximum of ten or twenty people at the workshop. To my amazement the auditorium was absolutely filled! Since we had not received an agenda before walking into the auditorium, imagine my surprise when the featured speaker of the workshop was Dr. Gladys T. McGarey a personal friend and physician for Dr. Kübler-Ross. She has written many books such as, The Physician Within and Living Medicine. For at least forty-five minutes she talked about energy, positive healing, and many ways we can connect to the Universal Energy Source (God) to help ourselves and to help others. She looks radiant, talks with such sincerity and grace and is ninety-years old! Listening to her was like reading parts of the incredible material produced by Dr. Kübler-Ross.

The other example of synchronicity happened about the same time. I was receiving additional training to be an Eleventh-Hour Program volunteer for a special program within the Hospice of the Valley organization. This is a unique service that works with patients who are very close to crossing over. The person who directs this program was explaining her initial experience with the program and mentioned that although she is now on staff she started out as a volunteer and worked on Sundays with — of all people — Dr. Kübler-Ross when she was in Hospice care in Scottsdale, Arizona. What amazing connections the Universe creates for us. It seems that Dr. Kübler-Ross's energy is as strong as ever and she is still getting her message out!

I expect and welcome synchronicity to happen in my life. I invite it in to confirm to me that the pathway I am on is the correct one for me. I know that I must remain centered by explaining to others my truth about this pathway and how each step seems to lead me forward in deepening my belief. I know that my story will help others. I no longer become evasive or hold back when asked about my belief, my work or this book. Everyone has a right to decide to accept or reject it. It will not change the truth for me. I choose to be of service to others and I purposely try to understand the beliefs and pathways they are on. When we realize that each of us has chosen this life for the lessons we need to learn it makes the saying don't judge until you have walked a mile in another person's shoes that much more meaningful. Keeping an open mind allows my belief system to become deeper, stronger and more beautiful — like a hybrid rose.

My Hope for You

S haring my spiritual truth and worldview has been both exciting and frightening. Sharing parts of my life, particularly where it relates to the conversations with my son has been difficult. I have bared my soul, so to speak. I have done this with one purpose in mind, to help those people who are so locked into grief that their life has stopped evolving. They are a shell of the person they once were before their loss. Their lives have been frozen in time like a video that is stuck on the pause command on the remote control. After a certain amount of time in the pause cycle the screen goes blank. No new images or information is forthcoming. I understand that there are people who are afraid to let go of the pain of grief because without it they feel they might have nothing left of their loved one. I understand this and desperately want to grab them and explain that they can have a significant part — the essence — of their loved one back by communicating in the now, rather than be relegated to remembering simply the 'what was' of their existence. Our loved ones who have passed on do not want us to keep grieving but to start living. I know it will be the hardest thing some of you have ever done. You now know that I talk from experience. If you will consciously work at letting go of the grief, and believe in the possibility of a higher level of connection it can happen for you as it did for me. The grief is blocking your energy and surrounding you with an impenetrable wall. Those we love on the other side are naturally on a higher vibrational level — after all they no longer have the events of the world or their bodies to weigh them down. When you have different vibrational levels, communication is impeded and can even be impossible. We can understand this easier by relating to tuning your radio to a particular station. We need to be on the exact frequency to eliminate the static to hear and understand clearly. We need to break down the wall of grief that surrounds us. We then will be able to raise our own vibrational level, our frequency, through what we think, say and feel. Demonstrating truth in all that we do and knowing that unconditional love is the most powerful emotion we can experience will then allow the connection to be made with our loved ones. Think of it simply as letting go and letting God or the Universe or whatever you choose to label the power greater than yourself take the weight of the heavy backpack filled with grief off your shoulders. After all, many of us have been taught to ask and you shall receive.

In writing this book, if I have helped even one person through the gripping stranglehold of grief from losing a loved one, then I will be thankful and feel I have been of service. There is no greater reward than to be of service to others. It makes the world a little better place. So tonight, after finishing this book you might consider listening to Handel's Messiah, the Hallelujah Chorus, then go outside and look up at the incredible work of our Universe and think of the stars as lights flickering on and off by our loved ones to let us know they are near us and happy since they are surrounded by the unconditional love of all who have gone before them and all who have yet to be with them. It is the true definition of infinity. They will keep the lights on as lanterns to guide us home to them, our true north, when our lessons are learned.

In closing, I would like to say "Thank you!" to my mom, Ronnie and sister for being with me every step of the way as I wrote this book. I hope I made you proud and it is all it is supposed to be. You remind me of the lyrics in the song, "Wind Beneath My Wings," by Bette Midler, "*I can fly higher than an eagle,*" because of your faith in me. I love you for all that you were and all that you are and all that you have yet to be. See you later and remember to keep the gate open for me!

ML

Epilogue

For the next few years the annual October Homecoming parade at our high school continued on with the 350 student marching band members leading it and playing the school fight song to elicit school spirit for the big football game that night. As the parade weaved its way through the winding streets of the community the canopies formed by the huge oak trees with their breathtaking red, yellow and orange colors added to the festivities. The administrators and board members sat on top of the back seats of the convertibles throwing candy to the children and community members who sat alongside the parade route in lawn chairs and blankets. Waving and cheering to us, they were definitely proud of their school system. The district had continued to excel. We graduated more students each year and the scholarships awarded to these students were becoming more and more substantial. This was truly Hometown, USA at its finest. Each year as I waved to these incredibly supportive community members, in my heart I would secretly be waiting for a special moment and a specific location just ahead on the route. As the parade veered to the right the home that I was watching for came into sight. Yes! There she was.

The mother of one of the students who had been killed in the car accident May 16, 1999 was outside on her porch, once again, watching the parade. After we exchanged waves I would put my hand on my heart as a signal to her that… I remembered…mother to mother.

After a few years the parade route had to be changed, according to the police department, due to safety issues – too much traffic now existed to march through the community. We needed to stay on the school property and devise a rather circuitous way to stage a parade. A wonderful tradition had ended. Just like everything in life change needed to happen. Although we would no longer be going by that special house, I knew in my heart that she would be thinking of us.

The memory of our sons would continue to surface in each others minds on this day as well as other significant days in our lives. The community, staff and parents had come to grips with the importance of moving on. They had wrapped their arms around us when we were at our most vulnerable. They helped us stand when we could no longer find the strength. We couldn't change the past – the loss would always be there. But just as the parade route had changed, our lives had also changed. We needed to honor the past, reinforce the importance of the present and dig deep into ourselves to visualize a more positive future. We were resilient and would survive. We had learned many lessons along this particular route in our lives.

Ronnie's boys are now in high school and their brother is just finishing his first year of college. They are doing well considering what they have been through. They lost their dad at such a young age. He loved them more than life itself. Ronnie's wife has resumed her volunteerism as a paramedic for the local fire department. She continues to share with the boys so much about their dad. He may physically be gone but he will never be forgotten. The memorial park that she created remains a living tribute to a man that had made his mark on this mountain community and on his family. The boys pass by it daily on their way to school.

As for me, I have learned so many lessons on this journey. However, a few stand out as show stoppers. The importance of listening with greater patience and empathy to someone as they struggle with life issues cannot be overstated. We have not walked in their shoes. We do not know their own special story. Visiting with Hospice patients who know they are facing a limited number of days left on this earth, I challenge myself to find little ways to bring joy to their moments. Being of service to others and making this place called earth a little better off when I leave it continues to be a motivating factor to me. Most importantly, learning that communication is never ending, regardless of what side of the door you may be on has been a monumental lesson. Love truly is the alpha and omega of the Universe.

Bibliography

Berstein, Judith R. 1997. *When the Bough Breaks Forever After the Death of a Son or Daughter.* Kansas City, Mo.: Andrews McMeel.

Browne, Sylvia. 2005. *Contacting Your Spirit Guides.* Carlsbad, Cal.: Hay House.

Browne, Sylvia. 2001. *Past Lives, Future Healing.* New York: Dutton

Callanan, Maggie and Patricia Kelley. 1997. *Final Gifts.* New York: Bantam

Chodron, Pema. 2000. *When Things Fall Apart.* Boston: Shambhala

Chopra, Deepak. 2001. *Soulmate.* New York: Putnam

Cockell, Jenny. 1996. *Past Lives, Future Lives.* New York: Fireside/ Simon Schuster

Collins, Kelsey. 2008. *Exit Strategy: Leaving this Life with Grace and Gratitude.* Sisters, Or.: ChaseHawk

Davis, T.J., Dianne Lane, and Barbara Joanne Walker. 1983. *Helen: A Psychic Gift.* Boulder, Co.; Brownsville

Eadie, Betty J. 1994. *Embraced by the Light.* New York: Bantam

Edward, John. 2000. *What if God Were the Sun?* San Diego, Ca.: Jodere Group

Edward, John. 2010. *Infinite Quest.* New York: Sterling

Gibran, Kahlil. 1957. *The Prophet.* New York: Knopf

Goodwin, Charlotte. 2008. *The Twisted Path.* Beaverton, Or.: Hideaway Press

Hanson, Warren. 1997. *The Next Place.* Golden Valley, Minn.: Waldman House Press

Hicks, Esther and Jerry. 2004. *Ask and It is Given.* Carlsbad, Ca.: Hay House

James, John W., and Russell Friedman. 2009. *The Grief Recovery Handbook.* New York: Harper Collins

Jaworski, Joseph. 1998. *Synchronicity: The Inner Path of Leadership.* San Francisco, Ca.: Berrett-Koehler

Karnes, Barbara. 2003. *The Final Act of Living.* Depoe Bay, Or.: Barbara Karnes

Kübler-Ross, Elisabeth. 1969. *On Death and Dying.* New York: MacMillan

Kübler-Ross, Elisabeth and David Kessler. 2005. *On Grief and Grieving.* Scribner New York: Scribner

_____, 2000. *Life Lessons.* New York: Scribner

Kübler-Ross, Elisabeth. 1995. *Death Is of Vital Importance.* New York: Station Hill

Kuman, Sameet M. 2005. *Grieving Mindfully.* Oakland, Ca.: New Harbinger

MacLaine, Shirley. 2011. *I'm Over All That.* New York: Atria

_____1990. *Going Within.* New York: Bantam

_____1986. *Out On A Limb.* New York: Bantam

_____2008. *Dancing In the Light.* New York: Bantam

_____2008. *Sage-ing While Age-ing.* New York: Atria

MacGregor, Trish and Rob MacGregor. 2010. *The 7 Secrets of Synchronicity.* Avon, Mass: Aadams Media

Martin, Joel and Patricia Romanowski. 2009. *Love Beyond Life.* New York: Harper

Medina, John. 2008. *Brain Rules.* Seattle, Wa.: Pear Press

Montgomery, Ruth. 1982. *Threshold To Tomorrow.* New York: Fawcett Crest

Moody Jr., Raymond A. 1975. *Life After Life and Reflections on Life After Life.* New York: Guideposts

Owusu, Hieke. 1999. *Symbols of Native America.* New York: Sterling

Peat, F. David. 1987. *Synchronicity/ The Bridge Between Matter and Mind.* New York: Bantam

Rand, Hollister. 2011. *I'm Not Dead, I'm Different.* New York: Harper

Redfield, James. 1993. *The Celestine Phrophecy.* New York: Warner

_____1996. *The Tenth Insight.* New York: *Warner*

_____1997. *The Celestine Vision.* New York: Warner

_____2011. *The Twelfth Insight.* New York: Grand Central

Rosof, Barbara D. 1994. *The Worst Loss.* New York: Henry Holt

Staudacher, Carol. 1994. *A Time To Grieve.* New York: Harper One

Van Vuken, John. 2000. *Edgar Cayce on the Revelation.* New York: Sterling

Van Praagh, James. 2001. *Healing Grief.* New York: New American Library

Ward, Suzanne. 2001. *Matthew, Tell Me About Heaven. Camas, Wa.: Matthew Books*

_____2002. *Revelations for a New Era.* Camas, Wa.: Matthew Books

_____ 2003. *Voices of the Universe.* Camas, Wa.: Matthew Books

_____2003. *Illuminations for a New Era.* Camas, Wa.: Matthew Books

Weiss, Brian L. 1992. *Through Time Into Healing.* New York: Fireside

_____ 2004. *Same Souls Many Bodies.* New York: Free Press

Wolterstorff, Nicholas. 1987. *Lament For A Son.* Grand Rapids, Mi.: Eerdmans

About the Author

Mary Leiker has spent her life developing others. As a teacher, counselor and superintendent, in Colorado and Michigan, she continued to share new ideas that would help others lead a more successful life.

Now, retired after 38 years in education, she has decided to share her life challenges, involving loss, in the hope that the lessons she has learned will be of benefit to others and give them strength. Mary has experienced innumerable losses in her life including death, divorce and suicide. Her greatest loss was that of her 36 year old son in May, 1999 from a tragic accident. She has been investigating the topic of grief and loss for over 30 years. It has been a passionate journey. In her book, JUST BEHIND THE DOOR, she shares a decade of transcribed communication from her son, mother and sister who have passed on. Her poignant story will give hope to those who are struggling and reassurance to those who are seeking answers to the tragedy of losing a loved one.

The door between our worlds is not intended to keep us separate from those who have passed on. The possibility of reconnecting with them while we are still on this earth is real and available to all of us, if we choose it. Our loved ones are eagerly waiting to have us open the our minds and reconnect with them!

Mary is now a Hospice volunteer and lives in Peoria, Arizona with her dog, Buddy.

CPSIA information can be obtained
at www.ICGtesting.com
Printed in the USA
FSOW01n1224290415
6804FS